World of Warcraft

World of Warcraft

Daniel Lisi

Boss Fight Books
Los Angeles, CA
bossfightbooks.com

ISBN 13: 978-1-940535-12-8
First Printing: 2016

Series Editor: Gabe Durham
Book Design by Ken Baumann
Page Design by Christopher Moyer

For Joe

CONTENTS

PART I: WHAT I TALK ABOUT WHEN I TALK ABOUT WARCRAFT

Hooked on a Feeling

IN AN AGGRESSIVELY HORMONAL and socially isolated stage of my life, I used *World of Warcraft* as a means of social connection, romance, entertainment, inspiration, and escape. When *WoW* came out on November 23, 2004, I was thirteen years old. I had been playing video games since the age of four, starting off my life-long passion with a Nintendo 64 console and all the greats of the time: *Super Mario 64*, *The Legend of Zelda: Ocarina of Time*, *Star Fox 64*, *Mario Kart 64*, and *GoldenEye 007*. Shortly after its release, *World of Warcraft* was installed and ready to play on my computer, and I was about to enter a world that would impact me for the rest of my life.

In my nine years of gaming, never before had I seen a single title take such a massive audience by storm. The MMO dominated gaming media, so much so that it merited the creation of news websites dedicated entirely to *World of Warcraft*. One of the more popular *WoW* news sources at the time, MMOChampion.com, started in 2007 and during *WoW's* prime brought in no fewer than ten million users a month.

The game soon burst out of its niche culture and into the mainstream, making headlines for its enormous financial achievement and its knack for drawing in gamers and non-gamers alike.

I was introduced to *World of Warcraft* by my stepdad Joe, a Navy man halfway through his two-year deployment in Okinawa, Japan when he met and married my mother. One afternoon, Joe took me to the mall on one of the first few one-on-one outings we had ever had: two strangers who were somehow required to build a parent-child relationship. He was eager to get on my good side, and I, as a manipulative thirteen-year-old, was eager to have him buy me shit.

We ended up in the EB Games store, and there it was: the game I'd been dying to play. "I've heard so much about this game!" I said, picking up the box of *EverQuest II*. Joe shook his head. "No, no," he said, handing me a different box, one with an angry-faced green creature on the front of it, *WORLD OF WARCRAFT* emblazoned in gold font. "Let's play this instead."

This was the fall of 2004. Joe was on a two-month leave, but he'd soon be returning to Okinawa. It was difficult connecting with Joe when there was such a huge distance between us physically and emotionally. My mother had remained a single parent for nearly twelve years after divorcing my biological father, so my new father figure had to find a way to break down some emotional walls to connect with me. Joe intended to use *World of Warcraft* as a tool to bond the two of us so that we could play together, chat, and continue the experience even when he was overseas.

And to that end, his plan succeeded. While Joe was overseas, *World of Warcraft* served as our primary means of communication. We'd log on and literally squat our characters down on a bench somewhere in one of Azeroth's grand cities and type away to each other. This method of bonding worked for us. We kept each other up to date and explored the fantasy realm quite a bit together, playing the roles of father and son in a virtual world.

But what Joe could not have predicted was that *World of Warcraft* would soon became a lifestyle for me. I eagerly avoided the eighth grade social world to spend more time in Azeroth, replacing outdoor activities and in-person hangouts with in-game events and dungeon raids. Eventually I joined a guild, a group of players who team up to face the game's tougher content, and my dedication for *WoW* only increased from there.

In other words, I'd bought into the full *World of Warcraft* experience, one that can be broken up into five phases:

1. Pay Blizzard. After purchasing the game client for $50, you must set up an online subscriber account that charges you a monthly fee of $15 to retain online access to the game.

2. Early-game. Pick a character faction. You can take sides with the mighty Horde or the honorable Alliance. Pick a character race. If you teamed up with the Horde during the classic unexpanded version of *WoW*, you could be a brutish Orc, a gangly and stoner-y Troll, a peaceful shamanistic Tauren, or one of the cursed Undead. If you took the Alliance route, you could be a run-of-the-mill xenophobic fantasy Human, a tall stoic Night Elf, a crafty Gnome, or your typical loud bombastic Dwarf. Finally, pick your class. Each faction has the Warrior, Mage, Warlock, Druid, Priest, Rogue, and Hunter to choose from. The Paladin used to be a class specific to the Alliance, and the Shaman used to be specific to the Horde, but Blizzard has since made all classes available to all factions.

3. Mid-game. The level cap before any of the expansions was 60. If you found yourself between levels 30 and 40, you had a pretty good sense of whether or not you were in it for the long haul. Statistically, players would drop off around this point if the game wasn't their cup of tea mechanically, or if they didn't have anyone to play with online. I was not a part of the minority that fell away, which brings us to…

4. End-game. Once you hit level 60 it was time to venture forth into the game's top-level dungeons. Dungeons are challenging areas where you take a party, a group of exactly five players, and send them into a dangerous zone to defeat its bosses and earn the dungeon's coveted rare items. These items are designed to make your character powerful enough to eventually face raid content. Raids are huge dungeons made for 40-player groups to combat against *World of Warcraft*'s toughest enemies. Nowadays raids only require between 10 and 25 players, but back in the un-expanded *World of Warcraft*, raids necessitated a group of 40 individuals to team up and not only play the game together, but effectively coordinate their efforts to operate as one unified monster-demon-zombie-whatever killing machine. This logistical terror is made less terrible via guilds, teams of players who raid together regularly. Guilds unify players with similar goals and playtimes, and allow players to anticipate each other's tactics and gameplay abilities, turning raids into both a team practice and the game itself. Third-party voice chat software (like Ventrilo or TeamSpeak) is often mandated across the guild so that these huge groups of players can communicate effectively in real-time. Some guilds are casual and face off against raid content only

once or twice a month. Others hold a strict daily schedule, which leads us to the final, optional tier of becoming a *WoW* player.

5. Hardcore players. To become the best a *World of Warcraft* server has to offer requires commitment. Hardcore raiding guilds—guilds that compete with one another on a national scale to clear end-game boss content before any other guild in the world (or on a smaller scale, their server)—spend up to six scheduled evenings a week, usually between four to six hours of game time per session, to progress through raid content. This race is tracked on the leaderboards of WoWProgress.com, a third-party website that displays every boss killed by every *WoW* guild on Earth.

I became a hardcore player. After Joe got me hooked, I spent the next three and a half years playing *WoW* with the same group of people, three to four nights a week, three to five hours a night. These were people I got to know intimately.

The vast multitudes of people playing *WoW* turned the game into a global cultural phenomenon, which in turn made excessive playing socially acceptable. At its peak, *World of Warcraft* held twelve million annual subscribers, almost half the entire population of Europe in the sixth century. And that is exactly what made *World of Warcraft* the *World of Warcraft* we know—people. Millions and millions of people.

The Genesis of Warcraft

On February 8, 1991, UCLA graduates Michael Morhaime, Frank Pearce, and Allen Adham founded Silicon & Synapse, a company that chiseled itself into the Blizzard Entertainment we know today, a developer of some of the world's largest video game franchises.

Blizzard released three titles under their old moniker of Silicon & Synapse: *RPM Racing*, *The Lost Vikings*, and *Rock n' Roll Racing*. After rebranding to Blizzard Entertainment in 1994, the company released another original title called *Blackthorne* and a contract project, *The Death and Return of Superman*, before hatching a game that would change the games industry forever: *Warcraft: Orcs & Humans*.

Warcraft: Orcs & Humans is a real-time strategy game that introduced us to the world of Azeroth for the very first time. The elevator pitch for *Warcraft*: Humans live on the planet Azeroth. The evil Orcs, fueled by bloodlust and strife, invade Azeroth via a portal from their home planet of Draenor, creating a culture of never-ending war between the two factions.

Warcraft became Blizzard's greatest financial and critical success yet. In November 1995 Entertainment Weekly reported that the game was ranked the 19th bestselling game across all categories that year. The success of *Warcraft* offered Blizzard a degree of financial stability and direction that hammered out the foundation for the mega-company that it is today.

After another contractual gig developing *Justice League Task Force*, Blizzard released the sequel for their budding franchise, *Warcraft II: Tides of Darkness*, on December 9, 1995. Mechanically, the game is a spitting image of *Warcraft*, offering the same user interface and array of gameplay mechanics, with some decently upgraded graphics. A review from *Computer Games Magazine* emphasizes that the sequel's AI systems "far surpassed that of the original game." When *Warcraft II* met with similar critical and financial success as the first *Warcraft*, Blizzard became as powerful of a development force as Westwood Studios, id Software, and LucasArts.

Blizzard Entertainment's development output between 1995 and 2002 was straight-up bonkers. After *Warcraft II*'s successful expansion, *Warcraft II: Beyond the Dark Portal*, Blizzard launched two more game-changing franchises with *Diablo* (1996) and *StarCraft* (1998), two games that deserve books themselves.

Before the release of *Warcraft III: Reign of Chaos* in 2002, Blizzard dropped a juicy nugget of news at the

European Computer Trade Show in September 2001: an MMORPG based in the *Warcraft* universe was coming to the PC.

Warcraft III became a massive critical and financial success, permitting the release of an expansion pack on July 1, 2003, *Warcraft III: The Frozen Throne*. At this point, *World of Warcraft* was roughly two to three years into development, using the proprietary elements of *Warcraft III*'s graphics engine to sculpt the aesthetic of the game.

After a total of four to five years of development and extensive testing, *World of Warcraft* released to the public on November 23, 2004, the 10th anniversary of the Warcraft franchise.

By 2005, *World of Warcraft* held 5,000,000 worldwide subscribers. By comparison, *EverQuest*'s subscription base had peaked at 450,000 in its lifetime. It was obvious that in just one year, *WoW* had launched an MMO—one of the more obscure genres in gaming—into what would become one of the most profitable assets in gaming history.

The three years spanning between 2007 and 2010 was when *World of Warcraft* ascended from niche culture popularity into the mainstream. *WoW* blazed trails through pop culture with commercials featuring celebrities like William Shatner and Aubrey Plaza and television shows like *South Park* dedicating episodes to the realm of Azeroth. Every other 7-Eleven snack food had a *World of Warcraft* theme attached to it, inspiring Mountain Dew to create their own themed flavors of soda: Alliance Blue and Horde Red.

Blue tasted better.

Azeroth in Decline

Since *WoW*'s player base peak in 2010, the MMO's population has had its ups and downs, influenced entirely by the introduction of new expansion packs. Millions of users taper off after five or six months of a new expansion and millions of users return the first month of a new expansion pack's release. The player base has tended to gravitate between eight to ten million users, until its record low in 2015 when the population sank to 5.6 million subscribers.

If you Google "is *World of Warcraft* dying," a significant number of results pop up for every single year since 2011. Countless articles have predicted the possible, eventual, and inevitable decline of the monolithic MMO.

The truth is: *World of Warcraft* has been "dying" since its launch day. The MMO is an organic creature, and its players are its blood. Every year there's a plethora of new content that augments the world and expands its depth, making it a more interesting, more complex ecosystem. The systems that were so fresh and groundbreaking years ago will lose their luster when compared to a generation of newer games.

A flashy new RPG will arrive, new consoles will release, and captivating experiences that demand attention will catch the user's eye and steal away another $15 subscription from Blizzard Entertainment. But judging by the three million subscriber uptick on *Warlords of Draenor*'s 2014 release, I think it's fair to say that all the player base wants is to be entertained by new things, even if *WoW*'s ability to satisfy those wants is constantly threatened by younger, flashier games.

World of Warcraft is simply dying of old age. In the world of technology and new media, a world that outdates and adapts itself swiftly and mercilessly, it has lived a remarkably long life, and is aging damn well considering that it still maintains a subscriber base that still trumps the peak base of most new MMOs. Like *EverQuest*, there will be active *WoW* servers for decades to come.

According to Blizzard at the time of this writing, two more expansions packs will release before Blizzard ceases spending development resources on *WoW*. *World of Warcraft: Legion*, *WoW*'s sixth expansion pack, is slated for release November 2016.

Whenever a glossy new cinematic trailer is released, I'm always tempted to return to Azeroth, to explore a world that I grew up in, that shared a huge part of my childhood. But playing *World of Warcraft* just isn't what I want out of a game anymore. My tastes have changed, and the MMO no longer fulfills me or entertains me. I aged alongside *World of Warcraft*. It is like a childhood pet that I once shared a deep bond with, but eventually had to put down and bury in the backyard.

The Mechanics of World of Warcraft

After creating an account with Blizzard Entertainment's battle.net and punching in your credit card number for the $15 monthly fee to play *World of Warcraft*, you're ready to log on, pick a server, and create your first character.

Mechanically, *World of Warcraft* follows the straightforward keyboard-and-mouse fantasy RPG play system adopted directly from *EverQuest*, and *Ultima Online* before that. The movement scheme is a standard WASD button layout, meaning you press W to move forward, A to move left, S to move right, and D to move backwards. You use the mouse to determine your camera direction, to interact with your environment, and to activate your abilities from a bar nesting an array of icons at the bottom of your screen.

After picking from between the nine class options and five races, you're given an array of aesthetic customization options to pick from. When you've settled on your looks and your name, your avatar is dropped into your race's specific starting zone to begin learning your class's basic abilities and the game's control mechanisms.

World of Warcraft takes place in the Tolkienesque planet of Azeroth. From the overworld, you can seamlessly explore a sprawl of rural landscapes and cities, only experiencing a loading screen when transitioning from one continent to another, or into a dungeon or raid.

To give some perspective into the size of *World of Warcraft*'s world, the Eastern Kingdoms, Azeroth's easternmost continent, is approximately twelve square miles of real-world equivalent playable terrain. Azeroth was enormous compared to other game worlds of its time, particularly to the worlds of more linear games that confined to very specific parameters. *World of Warcraft*'s borders are open and seamless, allowing for seemingly boundless exploration.

You initially progress through the game by defeating enemies and completing quests. Both of these actions grant you experience points that advance you to higher levels. The initial level cap of *World of Warcraft* was level 60, and it commonly took players an average of three months, at four to five hours of playtime a week, to reach this level. The game now, at its level cap of 105, has since found ways to expedite this process, even allowing players to purchase their way into higher levels in an intricate micro-transaction system.

As you progress in level, your character gains additional abilities depending on its class, and your playstyle adjusts to the role you choose to take. *World of Warcraft* originally had nine classes—Druids, Hunters, Mages, Paladins, Priests, Rogues, Shaman, Warlocks, and Warriors—and the expanded *WoW* now offers Death Knights and Monks. *Legion*, *WoW*'s forthcoming sixth expansion, will introduce the Demon Hunter as the game's twelfth playable class. These classes are partitioned into the three archetypes of RPG gameplay: DPS (Damage Per Second), tanks, and healers.

DPS classes are responsible for dealing out perfectly timed move combinations to inflict as much damage as possible against enemies. Despite individual visual styles and contextual mechanics that make each *World of Warcraft* boss unique, battles generally boil down to a race against the clock—kill the boss before the boss kills you. This means that formulaically optimizing the speed of your damage output is a necessity in later, harder game content.

Tanks are the classes responsible for attracting and absorbing most if not all incoming damage from enemies. They're given an array of abilities that generate "aggro," an internal metric that determines which player in a party the AI is going to attack first, so that the DPS and Healers are free to perform their duties without having to worry about incoming enemy damage.

Healers meanwhile hold the group together by replenishing members' depleted hit points. If the party dynamics are in correct order, healers typically focus their healing powers on the tank, who receives the most incoming damage.

Early on in the game's progression you gain access to your class's "talent tree," choosing from one of three paths and then allocating "talent points" to specify your class role according to your own tastes. This allows for most classes, barring some specialists, to focus on DPS, tanking, or healing. For example, a "Warrior" is a common tanking class. If you wanted to focus on the tanking element of gameplay, you'd allocate your talent points (or "spec") in the "Protection" tree.

Alternatively, if charging into the fray and decapitating your enemies with a humongous two-handed great sword was more your style, you could then spec into "Fury" and become a DPS warrior instead. Spending talent points in your talent tree and gaining further class abilities are the only two things that change the game mechanically as you progress forward, allowing you a wider selection of actions to perform in any given combat scenario.

The next stage in *World of Warcraft*'s early gameplay is delving into dungeons with a group of four other players. Dungeons are separated from the public overworld by the creation of "instances," private areas that remain exclusive to the group of players entering them for the duration of their mission. When a party enters a dungeon, an exclusive version of that dungeon is created just for those five players. This allows the group to progress at its own pace, and to prevent other players from interfering with the challenge of that dungeon.

Running a dungeon is a hugely social task. And whereas most dungeons today take about half an hour to complete, many dungeons in the original *WoW* took a full two hours. If your tank, healer, or DPS are not pulling their weight, a party can take hours longer than what would normally be required to defeat (or "clear") a dungeon's content. A good party member in this early stage can become a friend to hit the dungeons with again, and can even eventually lead to a guild invite.

A party member's reliability is quantifiable. If you don't do your job well—keeping enemies off the rest of the party, keeping the tank alive, or quickly dispensing of enemies—you'll risk losing allies for future missions or be bullied by your party's other players.

The benefit of spelunking into these dungeons is the promise of new equipment. Equipment in *World of Warcraft* is broken up into six tiers:

- Poor Quality: Denoted with grey text. Good only for selling to NPCs for chump change.
- Common Quality: Denoted with white text. The type of gear your character starts out with.
- Uncommon Quality: Denoted with green text. The type of equipment that will stick with you for the first few levels, but will quickly become obsolete when you begin dungeon content.
- Rare Quality: Denoted with blue text. The type of gear bosses will drop inside of dungeons, or as a reward for turning in difficult quests.
- Epic Quality: Denoted with purple text. The gear you'll find defeating raid bosses, and what hardcore raiders strive to garb their characters in.
- Legendary Quality: Denoted with orange text. The best of the best. Back in the day, there were only two legendary weapons in the game, and you'd be able to count on two hands the number of people on a server who had them.

These mechanics as I've explained them create the meat of *World of Warcraft*'s gameplay. On paper, *WoW* sounds like a game I'd play for a week or two before scuttling off to binge on the next game like the insatiable cultural vampire I am. What, then, made us players return again and again to *World of Warcraft* so compulsively?

PART 2:
A PORTRAIT OF THE RAIDER AS A YOUNG MAN

The Escapist

I WAS PARTICIPATING IN A RAID on the shadowy tower of Karazhan with nine of my fellow guildmates when I told my stepfather to go fuck himself. He was in my room asking me to turn off the computer and enjoy a nice day in the park with the family, the kind of scheduled outing that I used to crave, and instead of agreeing I lashed out like the angsty teen I was. Immediately after, I stared up at him goggle-eyed, feeling shocked at my own absurdity, immediately predicting the ramifications of my blatant disregard for parent-child dynamics.

To understand why I lashed out, you must first understand how deeply I'd bought in.

One of the first changes made to the original *World of Warcraft* (or "vanilla *WoW*") in *WoW*'s first expansion was the reduction of raiding parties from 40 members to 25. This created a much more intimate environment amongst teammates. Nobody was superfluous; everyone needed to carry their weight or the entire operation would stall like a Rube Goldberg machine missing a domino.

As a result of the change, guilds took extensive measures to screen new raiding members to ensure they were not bringing on any dead weight, or as hardcore raiders like to call them, "scrubs." To even get to a point where I qualified for an interview with a guild, I had to reach level cap (one month of gameplay, averaging 20 hours a week), play through lower-difficulty dungeons to acquire enough gear on my own to reach minimum levels of damage per second to prove a viable asset to the raid (another month), and finally join the guild on a probationary basis to show that they could get along with me personally (one final month). This process—more demanding than landing yourself an entry-level job—is what separated me from the casual arena of *World of Warcraft*.

I went through three interviews, one with the guild master, one with my class leader (I played a rogue), and finally one with the raid leader—the fella whose job it was to read any and all material on boss encounters, teach us the raid the mechanics of every encounter, then call the shots during the encounter itself. The skillset required to be a good raid leader is rather impressive. You have to give commands from a core set of knowledge on an improvised basis depending on the actions of 24 other people. Having the proper reaction to all of those contingencies was what made a good raiding guild good, and often earned the raid leader the respect of his or her comrades.

Through no small effort I made the cut. I was now a member of a prestigious raiding guild. According to the journal I kept the summer of 2005, this was my proudest achievement to date, usurping my first place trophy from the 2003 AYSO soccer league.

Two of my real-life friends were a part of this guild, and my acceptance did wonders for our bond. We went from hanging out on campus with mutual friends to exclusively seeing each other on a daily basis, hanging out after school, and taking midnight trips to Denny's after binging on *WoW* for hours. Eventually my commitment to the guild surpassed even theirs, and I developed a closer affinity with my online guildmates than I had with them. My real-life friends moved on to a more casual guild while I continued in the arena of the hardcore raider.

From my parents' perspective, red flags about my relationship with *World of Warcraft* started appearing long before I told my stepdad to go fuck himself. A few months after I had started playing in 2004, I skipped Rosh Hashanah. Instead of celebrating the Jewish New Year with my mother, four aunts, six cousins, and a gaggle of family friends, I stayed home to play *WoW*. My mother was livid. Joe made an international call from Okinawa to ask me why I decided against spending time with my family that evening. It bothered me that Joe had called me instead of messaging me in-game. I told him about my discomfort with family gatherings, and that I'd rather be playing *WoW* than blowing on a shofar.

More than anything, I found it necessary to impress my guildies. There was trust placed in me to perform my job, a job I'd spent weeks studying for and grinding toward. I often think about the amount of time I spent on this goal, searching for some kind of silver lining, some kind of skill that I refined that I now apply to my everyday life. I am sure my stepfather, moments after being cussed at by a kid in his care, was asking himself the same thing. What could his stepson be deriving from such a prolonged exposure to *WoW*? At the time, all that mattered was the impression I'd leave on my companions if I abandoned them mid-raid.

In Mario Lehenbauer-Baum and Martina Fohringer's paper "Towards Classification Criteria for Internet Gaming Disorder: Debunking Differences Between Addiction and High Engagement in a German Sample of *World of Warcraft* Players," the authors point out that while we humans have become good at identifying substance addiction in one another (loss of control, withdrawal symptoms, and negative consequences in school, the workplace, and in relationships), we are much less experienced in recognizing addiction to online games. The addiction, like gaming itself, is simply too new.

The role of researchers like Lehenbaur-Baum and Fohringer, then, is to identify what being "addicted to games" actually looks like. The paper's study focuses on the divide between players who are highly engaged with *World of Warcraft* but are still capable of maintaining their responsibilities in the real world and a minority of players that "seem to have problems with a healthy amount of gaming."

I was a member of the latter group. And while no term for my affliction existed at the time, the American Psychiatric Association in 2013 introduced "Internet Gaming Disorder" (IGD) to the fifth edition of the Diagnostic and Statistical Manual of Mental Disorders (DSM-5)—the psychiatrist's bible of mental disorders—as a "Condition for Further Study."

When I recently asked Joe what he thought eight years ago when I told him to go fuck himself, he told me that I reacted how any addict reacts when his vice is threatened.

Joe's solution was to ban me from *World of Warcraft*. I didn't take the news well. I claimed that my life would be devoid of any joy, that this was all I had. These claims only solidified my stepfather's understanding that I was addicted to *World of Warcraft*.

At the time, I really didn't think I could get by without *WoW*. As a five-foot kid with a love for fantasy and computers, I practically had a target painted on my back for bullies. The MMO was my salvation. Joining an online community under a fantastical new identity was a safe reprieve from schoolyard torment. Besides, everything online seemed to be just as fulfilling as anything the real world had to offer.

Perhaps what Joe saw in me was a stark reflection of his own tousles with escapism. Joe, in the midst of his duties in Japan, was in a place of mighty uncertainty and rapid change. All within a year's time he found himself with a new wife, a sudden pregnancy, and a stepson he was expected to father. Joe was only 24 years old, as old as I am now writing this book. Video games remained a static, relaxing certainty in his life, and his own commitment to *WoW* often matched my own.

My first brush with gaming addiction was on a virtual pet website called Neopets. I owe my full-stack web development abilities to constructing and maintaining an online storefront where I specialized in selling paintbrushes to beautify the Neopet world's adorable digitized companions.

The primary draw of Neopets, like that of *World of Warcraft*, was its community. I was able to relate to and share with people my age without any social risk. Under the safety blanket of the internet, I got to build new personas, accentuating the aspects of myself that I liked (my craftiness, wit, and aptitude for storytelling) while burying those that made me insecure (my physicality, my frizzy Jew-fro) behind the abstraction of an avatar. I hoped that maybe someday the idealistic avatars I created would somehow replace my real self.

In 2012, three researchers from University of Hamburg's Institute of Social Psychology published an article titled "The Social Side of Gaming: How Playing Online Computer Games Creates Online and Offline Social Support." The study sought to discover whether a social life built on an online game's community could be as fulfilling as a social life born of in-person interactions.

After surveying 811 online gamers, the authors concluded that online gaming may indeed result in strong social ties between gamers playing the game together, but that the gamers generally only reach a level of deep social fulfillment if the relationship extends beyond the game world and into the real one.

Mechanically, *World of Warcraft* is a formulaic numbers-based RPG that relies solely on stat-boosting, gear-building, and farming the same or similar content in hopes of getting a brief spurt of euphoria brought on by epic-rated items. Compared to a solo sandbox game like *The Elder Scrolls V: Skyrim*—with its lush world, fully voiced-over dialogue, and vast possibility space— *World of Warcraft*'s gameplay has been engineered to run on rails. Any of the variance in *WoW*'s gameplay comes from the people you encounter it with.

The Design of a Hardcore Raider

In his 1961 book *Man, Play, and Games*, sociologist Roger Caillois states that "[p]lay is an occasion of pure waste: waste of time, energy, ingenuity, skill, and often money." He adds that games are also a source of joy, as well as a healthy means of escape from responsibility and routine, but must adhere to a set of rules to reach a healthy balance.

Caillois offers such a set of rules for making games. According to Caillois, a game must create a carefree space in which the player feels free from obligation, must not bleed into the player's "real life," must not offer the player certain success, must not be a "productive" activity but must exist for its own sake, must be governed by clear and discernible rules, and must be rooted not in reality but make-believe. These are rules I follow when making my own games.

In *The Burning Crusade*, *WoW*'s first expansion, Blizzard introduced "daily quests"— tasks that can be completed on a daily basis to earn the same reward each time, usually a sum of in-game currency and "reputation points," a metric used to determine your standing amongst in-game factions. Once your reputation reached the maximum with a faction, you gained access to powerful enchantments and items that sometimes proved vital to end-game players.

This feature obliges players to check back in on a daily basis to meet standards that were being set by raiding guilds, adding yet another necessary task to keep up with being a good guild member—breaking one of Caillois's rules for play.

For many hardcore raiders, myself included, raiding started to feel like a second job. The social obligation and the risk of being removed from your role in a guild motivates hardcore players to return to the game on a habitual, regimented basis. The chance at better equipment and the opportunity to see game content unfold was only possible when you clocked in every day. Your commitment, then, is not to the game itself but to your community.

This is no accident. In the 2011 book *Building Successful Online Communities*, the authors of a chapter called "Encouraging Commitment in Online Communities" advise that community designers "make design decisions that influence whether and how people will become committed to a community," noting that "[c]ommitted members work harder, say more, do more, and stick with a community after it becomes established. They care enough to help with community activities and to sustain the group through problems."

In *WoW*, the more work you put into raiding, the more content your guild unlocks and the better gear your team acquires. As Paul McCartney wrote in "The End": "And in the end, the love you take, is equal to the love you make"—just replace the first "love" with "gear" and the second "love" with "raids."

And raids are not just played but studied. We always knew about the raid bosses we were to encounter, even if it was our first time facing them. Every item a boss could yield was calculated down to the percentage rate of their dropping. Updates on raid content were carefully spaced out just enough so that when the majority of guilds had cleared a current patch's raid, new content was around the corner.

Hardcore raiding schedules turn an otherwise unproductive "leisure" activity into a competitive sport, whether you're "only" vying for supremacy on your server like we were or competing internationally against top-tier guilds. The rules of the game at this level weren't only set by Blizzard developers but also by the *WoW* community itself. The obligations and stresses of *World of Warcraft* were created by us.

Alex Golub's 2010 article "Being in the World (of Warcraft): Raiding, Realism, and Knowledge Production in a Massively Multiplayer Online Game," outlines this progression succinctly:

> These instances generally follow a certain "pro-gression": you must kill all of the bosses in one instance before you can kill the bosses in another instance. A guild's success and seriousness is

measured by how far it has "progressed" in "end-game content." It is this goal of progression that is shared by guild members. For instance, in *WoW* 2.0 players must slay Gruul and Magtheridon before moving on to Serpentshrine Cavern, where they must slay five bosses before finally taking down Lady Vashj. After this, players may advance to Tempest Keep, kill the three bosses there, and then take down Kael'thas Sunstrider, the final boss. Once Vashj and Kael are "down," players are "attuned" to The Battle of Mount Hyjal, where there are four bosses to kill before taking down Archimonde. Only then may players proceed to the Black Temple, where there are eight bosses to kill before facing lllidan Stormrage, the final boss in *WoW* 2.0.

Exodus, one of *World of Warcraft's* highest-ranked raiding guilds, disbanded in 2013. Shortly after, in a Facebook post dated April 26, 2013, guild leader Killars spoke out about the guild's dissolution: "It's certainly becoming a more difficult breed to be a part of. What I mean by this is of course the time commitment and the level of sheer dedication and determination it takes and costs to be at the very top... Unfortunately we (hardcore raiders) pushed too hard. Tier after tier we just keep adding to the insanity in both farming preparations and actual progressing. It's almost as if progression itself never really ends after an end tier boss dies. Combine this with Blizzard actually putting new content out faster, alts playing a big role, PTR/BETA, dailies, coins, BMAH, well... you just get lost in it all."

This level of intensity is, of course, not shared by every single raiding guild in *World of Warcraft*. However, the behaviors do repeat themselves enough across guilds and across servers to show a trend in the type of culture and ideology created by hardcore players. The result is a vicious cycle of addictive behavior that is spurred on by a group of enablers—twenty-four other guildmates participating in the same guild culture.

World of Warcraft's original raiding content was arguably the most demanding on its players, requiring the 40-person raiding teams to log countless hours progressing through content. On his blog Hardcore Casual, *WoW* player SynCaine wrote a post in 2007 titled "Looking in the Mirror; the Sickness that Was *WoW* Raiding." The author was the main tank for a top-tier raiding guild, as well as an officer in the guild's hierarchy. The guild raided six nights a week, starting around 7 p.m. and ending around 1 or 2 a.m.

SynCaine talks about how he provided additional hours around his raiding schedule to provide upkeep and preparation support to the guild and its raids, and only missed a raid if he "was on vacation (rare) or due to some emergency (also rare)," adding, "I planned movies/dates/dinners/etc. around raids."

SynCaine's raiding attendance was around 90-95%, but regardless of his effort and the amount of hours he spent outside of raiding, he writes:

> I always felt I could be doing more, that our guild was not progressing fast enough, that we were not learning encounters as quickly as we should be, or that our membership was not stable enough to push faster. I spent a good amount of time on our guild forums discussing ways to improve our progress and increase our pace. I remember getting frustrated with members who would not log on consistently, or who had to leave a raid halfway in. We knew exactly who our best healer/DPS/support players were; we had the guild all-stars and we had the rest. I could take one look at a raid and know if we had a chance for progress or not, simply based on how many of our 'key' players were on that night. The players who, like me, were consistently online and put in the extra effort to read up on strategies and farm up potions/buff items. It was a constant effort to find those types of players to replace those that 'only' raided 3-4 nights a week, those that did not

put in the 2-3 hours to farm up potions or read extensive strategy write-ups.

Whenever I did miss a raid, I would hear about it the next day; and at worst find out that the raid had not gone as planned due to lacking a tank. This guilt factored in heavily in making me log on. I felt that if I take a night off, I would be letting 39 others down, people who depended on me to be there. [...] Most of all, I did not want to act like the people who I was trying to remove, the 'casual' raiders who did not dedicate 5-7 nights a week to the guild.

The game became a stressful obligation rife with social dependencies and pressure. What ended up getting to SynCaine, though, was simply boredom. Eventually, clearing the same content with the same people week after week got stale. A full-sized *World of Warcraft* raid typically housed eight to ten bosses, and took around two months to clear fully.

Some bosses took many attempts to defeat. For instance, the first boss in Blackwing Lair, a dragon named Razorgore the Untamed, took my guild nearly two weeks to conquer. When a boss defeats an entire raid party, it is referred to as a "raid wipe." Whether it was poor party composition, ineffective leadership, or just insufficient understanding of a boss's mechanics, your entire evening in a raid could be spent wiping over and over again on a single encounter.

If a raiding group was frequently successful in defeating the bosses of a raid, the group would return every week to face the same content (or "farm" the content) to continue beating the encounters they became increasingly familiar with so that they could obtain all of the items that a boss could possibly drop. Epic-rated items that drop off of bosses have a degree of scarcity to them regardless of a party's ability to defeat a boss consistently, with each item generally having a 10-15% drop rate. This kind of scarcity made it worthwhile for guilds to return on a regular basis to defeat bosses they've already experienced.

Item scarcity made it so no player could get fully equipped in his or her optimal raiding equipment with only one successful raid clear. It took at least a month of very lucky drops, and even then you'd have to compete against other players in your guild who could also use the same equipment.

Because of item scarcity, guilds created ingenious internal economies completely independent of *World of Warcraft*'s mechanics to determine who should receive items dropped by raid bosses. The first system for fairly distributing items in MMOs was the application of Dragon Kill Points, or DKP, in *EverQuest* to deal with the game's similarly scarce drops among large-scale raid bosses that required many players to defeat.

The rules for DKP distribution varied from guild to guild, but in a nutshell, if you attended a raid on time, participated in the defeat of a boss, and remained in the raid until the very end, you received a number of DKP. When an item you desired dropped, a DKP bid would ensue and the player with the highest bid received the item.

If a guild established an internal DKP economy, the "currency" could then also be used as a means of punishment. If you somehow impeded the raid's progress, it was common for an angry raid leader to dock your DKP—which essentially amounted to your paycheck. If you performed well, you got a pat on the back with some points to buy goodies. If you did poorly, you got squat. This internal economy only intensified the demanding environment of hardcore raiding guilds. Furthermore, players who receive many items from a guild are often expected to remain loyal to the guild, becoming key members of a group. Pressure to remain active is common in *WoW* raiding guild culture.

SynCaine eventually quit his raiding guild. "I had had enough," he wrote, "and I realized, sadly so so late, that *WoW* was now 99% job, 1% fun for me. The only time I really enjoyed myself was when we downed a boss for the first time, and that happened perhaps once every two weeks or so. Near the end, everything else was work. Dealing with guild drama, judging new recruits, repeating a strategy in raid chat for the 1000th time, updating DKP, it was all work."

The desire of more casual players to raid and experience *World of Warcraft*'s endgame content has, fortunately, led to a decrease in time commitment as the expansion packs have progressed. *Burning Crusade* reduced raiding parties from forty players down to either ten-player groups or the slightly more challenging twenty-five-player groups, making assembling a raid far less logistically intensive.

When *WoW*'s third expansion, *Cataclysm*, arrived, a new "Looking for Raid" tool changed raiding forever by allowing players to enter a cross-server pool of people wanting to face raid content. The tool would then construct a balanced group and send them off to an easy-mode version of the raid, allowing players to experience the same boss encounters and receive slightly lower-quality versions of the most contemporary raiding equipment.

Combined with the easier raid bosses and comparable raiding equipment, the "Looking For Raid" tool lowered the barrier to raiding considerably, and made clearing raid content a casual endeavor. Players can now experience the entirety of an expansion's raiding content within a few hours where it used to necessitate months of time and dedication—a healthy step for *World of*

Warcraft players toward Roger Caillois's ideal of play for its own sake and away from obligation.

The LFR tool received a lot of backlash from hardcore raiding communities, stating that it undermined the existence of hardcore raiding guilds, that the game had become "too easy" in the wake of their hard work. Others found this to be an opportunity to finally quit their intense commitments to their guildmates, returning to what *WoW* likely was for them initially—a fun game.

The Second Best

Wrath of the Lich King, *World of Warcraft*'s second expansion pack, was released on November 13, 2008. The summer prior to its release, my raiding guild cleared Black Temple and the Sunwell, the two end-game raids of the *Burning Crusade* expansion pack, every single week in hopes of obtaining the last pieces our mathematically proven "best" equipment sets. For the rogues of the guild, this included two legendary drops off the final boss of Black Temple: Illidan Stormrage's twin Warglaives of Azzinoth. Unlike other RPGs where you can earn a pair of gloves or gauntlets as one item, in *WoW* you've got to find and equip each one separately—which meant that the Warglaives of Azzinoth were only available individually as main-hand and off-hand models.

A rogue lucky enough to beat the odds of both Warglaives' 5% drop chance and obtain the dual weapons would have the statistically greatest DPS weapons on the face of Azeroth. My guild sported two "core" team rogues, a guild veteran—let's call him "Pumpernickel"—and myself. Pumpernickel outranked me, and had been a part of the guild for about a year longer than I had. He had the main-hand Warglaive, and by merit of this had the rights to the off-hand Warglaive should it drop, as completing the set increased overall raid DPS rather than allowing another rogue a shot at the incomplete set.

Pumpernickel was absent the night the off-hand Warglaive dropped due to an unexpected medical emergency. The legendary weapon deferred to me, which suddenly made my character one of the two most well-equipped DPS-ers on the server, second only to Pumpernickel by 0.6%. I'd like to say that I didn't care about these statistics, but boy did I care. I cared a whole lot. As I've said, the game to me had evolved from entertainment into a competitive obligation. My rank on the server was an affirmation of my time and energy, and gained me the praise and respect of my peers. Becoming the second greatest rogue on the server meant that I had become a cherished asset to the people that I'd grown to care about and depend on.

This turned our weekly clearing of the raid dungeon of Black Temple into a white-knuckled gauntlet of anxiety. Every week Illidan Stormrage died the same dramatic death and the raid scrambled to the corpse of our fallen enemy to pilfer our rewards. Every week Pumpernickel hoped for the Off-hand Warglaive and I hoped for the Main-hand Warglaive. Every week it failed to appear in the dead boss's loot inventory. I refused to miss a single raid every week leading up to *Wrath of the Lich King*'s release in November out of fear that I would miss out on the Main-hand Warglaive drop. This trend repeated itself until the last week of September, when our guild's third and final Warglaive dropped—but it wasn't the one I needed.

The Off-hand Warglaive made its way into Pumpernickel's inventory, and thus his ranking as the server's top rogue solidified. I returned to the game's hub city of Shattrath to watch our guild enchanter bless the weapon with a Mongoose enchantment, which grants the user +25 to Agility on a random hit with the weapon it is enchanted with. He stood on top of a mailbox in the middle of the city like an asshole, dancing with his weapons drawn for the entire online population to see.

With *Wrath of the Lich King*, the level cap raised from 70 to 75, and I quickly replaced my level 70 legendary Off-hand Warglaive of Azzinoth with a higher-level (but uncommon-grade) dagger called the Ominous Dagger of the Owl from a quest that made me dispatch ten viking-esque enemies in the newly accessible continent of Northrend. I deposited the expended legendary that I'd spent months obsessing over into my bank to look back on and remember.

Soon my entire level 70-optimized raiding set made its way into my character's storage: Gear of legendary quality was quickly outmoded by new gear that was graded merely uncommon. The cycle I put myself through in the *Burning Crusade* repeated in *Wrath of the Lich King*. I hit the level cap, then started grinding out dungeon content with some of my guildies to get enough rare-level gear to produce enough DPS for the new forthcoming raids.

The guild went back into a full-time raiding schedule as soon as enough of the core group was at maximum level and suited up in enough level 75 dungeon gear. The same covetous feelings came over me when browsing the potential item drops from bosses, and I hit the spreadsheets to calculate what gear would optimize my character's damage output.

New patches arrived, new raids with better equipment became available, and within a few weeks most of my painstakingly curated set from the previous raid's coffers ended up back in my storage vault alongside sets of armor that were no longer useful to me or my guild, tiny digital mementos of my obsession.

PART 3:
LOVE IN THE TIME
OF BLIZZCON

Margot

WHEN I WAS FIFTEEN YEARS OLD—two years into playing *World of Warcraft*—a digital flirtation struck up between me and a healer in my guild named Margot. It started as most online romances do, a few small-talk messages sent back and forth. Because I was a stupid fifteen-year-old, my contributions to these early conversations likely amounted to something like, "Yeah, I hate school!" and "Yeah, I'd rather be playing *World of Warcraft* instead of going to school!" But these messages eventually led to a more personal dialogue.

Margot became one of my first crushes. Through months of raiding and chatting, I came to know Margot, a seventeen-year-old from the UK, better than anyone in my immediate social circle, both offline and online. We confided in each other about our problems—my run-ins with bullies, the limits of her small town, and both of our conflicts with our families. I didn't yet know how to communicate all my teenage frustration and insecurity to my family, so being able to speak to someone on my wavelength who was not at all alienated by my binge-playing *WoW* was a huge relief. Margot and I bonded deeply over the escape we shared.

Relationships born online are increasing exponentially in social acceptance as our access to and immersion in the internet continues to grow. Findings published in the journal *Proceedings of the National Academy of Sciences* state that almost 35% of married couples have met online, with about 45% of those couples having met on dating sites. This research was gathered based on a survey of more than 19,000 individuals who married between 2005 and 2012.

It is no surprise then that *World of Warcraft*, with its lengthy raiding schedules and necessity for intimate cooperation, has led to some romantic encounters. Despite the stigma of video games being primarily an outlet for nerdy dudes, the Entertainment Software Association's statistics from 2004 to 2016 have reported that women consistently make up 38% or more of the population of gamers, with adult women over age 35 comprising exactly half of the game-playing demographic as of 2016. Games research firm Newzoo, meanwhile, reports that as as of mid-2015, 35% percent of *WoW* players are female, up from 29% in 2014. *WoW*'s 7.1 million user base dwarfs Match.com's two million subscribers, and *WoW* players already have a common interest. While there is no telling exactly how many relationships or marriages sprung from *World of Warcraft*'s servers, there are enough stories out there to infer that quite a few couples owe their romance to *WoW*.

Stephanie Rosenbloom's 2011 New York Times article "It's Love at First Kill" tells the tale of the budding romance of two *WoW* players: "It began on a hot summer night in Santa Barbara, California, when Tamara Langman helped kill the yellow-eyed demon known as Prince Malchezaar. She was logged into *World of Warcraft*, the multiplayer fantasy game, and her avatar—Arixi Fizzlebolt, a busty gnome with three blond pigtails—had also managed to pique the interest of John Bentley, a.k.a. Weulfgar McDoal."

Rosenbloom continues, "And so Ms. Langman and Mr. Bentley found a quiet spot for their avatars to sit. Hours evaporated as they discussed everything from their families to their futures. Sometime before dawn, Ms. Langman realized that while she was in the fictional world of Azeroth, she was also on a date."

The story goes on to describe how the two chatted in this fashion for months before he visited her for a two-week vacation that turned into a two-year relationship. "[*World of Warcraft* is] giving people something that they're missing in the real world," says Ramona Pringle, an interactive media producer and a professor, in the same article. "It is a really primal experience. It's about survival. It's about needing someone."

My mildly romantic friendship with Margot only increased my addiction to *World of Warcraft*. The incentive to play the game alongside Margot heavily outweighed any rewarding feelings I got from the real world. Not only did I have a group of peers who respected the work I did with them—I had a girlfriend. I had someone who listened to me and, without judgment, related to me. And I could do the same with her.

I was in a completely different world, detached from the social hysteria emanating from my high school. It almost felt as if I no longer needed the acceptance of my real-life peers. I could avoid the social ambiguity and awkwardness of face-to-face encounters, leaping directly into a place that felt safe and comfortable. An evening spent playing *World of Warcraft* made far more sense than another school dance.

Margot and I exchanged numbers, taking a step away from the abstraction of our avatars. I'd spend moments between classes texting her, and she got into the pattern of calling me after school. The best part of my day was spent walking the two-mile bike path home, talking to Margot on the phone and anticipating the moment when I could get home, throw off the weight of the day like a heavy coat, and log onto *World of Warcraft*.

Our conversations diverged from *WoW* and nerd culture into more personal areas. We started to understand each other's family lives, and shared our creative projects with each other—she wrote fan fiction stories depicting our guild's *WoW* characters, and I drew cruddy comic books and wrote terrible poetry.

World of Warcraft and Margot's affection allowed me to sweep the unprocessed pain of my daily teenage life under the rug. I didn't have to address the growing emotional distance between me and my parents or worry about my isolated nature at school. Here I could cut loose and be myself.

It never occurred to me that I could actually meet Margot in real life. Flying across the world to meet a girl I met online seemed like a logistical impossibility. Then, seemingly out of nowhere, Margot told me she was flying to California to go to BlizzCon 2007, the annual *World of Warcraft*-centric convention at the Anaheim Convention Center, only a twenty-minute drive from my hometown of Irvine. Margot and I made plans to meet at the convention. I was terrified.

The first BlizzCon was held in October 2005. I attended its pilot year with my biological father, an old-fashioned fella who still has never created an email address and refuses to learn how to text. He was in for a culture shock. This first year of BlizzCon required only one hall of the Anaheim Convention Center to host its 8,000 attendees. The convention had the campy air of a small community embracing their niche fandom. There was a mechanical bull akin to *WoW*'s Tauren, a bipedal bull-like species in Azeroth. My dad was horribly confused by all of it.

Come BlizzCon 2007, *World of Warcraft* maintained a subscription base of ten million annual users and had sold 2.4 million units of its first expansion within 24 hours of its release. *World of Warcraft* was no longer a hidden subculture. Blizzard now sold out their entire reservoir of 13,000 BlizzCon badges at $150 a badge in less than ten minutes.

BlizzCon's largest attendance to date was 27,000 attendees in 2010. This was the same year that *WoW* reached its highest subscription base at twelve million users. The convention has since plateaued at around 26,000 attendees annually. As Blizzard's cultural weight increased, BlizzCon drew increasingly popular musicians. Performers like Ozzy Osbourne, Blink-182, and Foo Fighters took the place of their developer-led band, Elite Tauren Chieftain, which played every year for the first three years.

Margot and a handful of my guildmates booked their rooms at a Radisson across the street from the Anaheim Convention Center. In total, there were four rooms on the same floor housing twelve core members of our guild. My guildies and I made plans to bring our computers for an in-hotel LAN party so that we could tackle a raid in the same room together.

Meanwhile, I was scrambling to find a way to make myself more presentable to Margot. It had never before occurred to me that she might not be attracted to me. Sure we had exchanged photos, but I only felt bold enough to send her pictures that had undergone extensive scrutiny and a forensic-like identification of the best camera angle for the shape of my head. Was it proportional to the rest of my body? Don't men have sharp jawlines? How can I make it so I look like I have more jawlines? I didn't know what attractive was, let alone how to present myself as such. I thought about stylish clothes for the first time in my teenage years. I needed a haircut. I felt too short. My insecurities that the internet so expertly concealed were all going to be revealed.

BlizzCon is a beautiful, tangible manifestation of *WoW* culture, enabling and underscoring what makes this MMO and others so successful—its social nature. BlizzCon sported a lounge area in the middle of the hall dotted with two-dozen island tables. Every hour, in alphabetical order, signs with names like "Moon Guard" or "Doomhammer" were placed on each table. This was where you'd go to meet people from the server you played on.

My impression was that the majority of groups roving the halls of BlizzCon were doing the same thing that I was doing—meeting with a core group of friends made online and cruising the convention halls with them in packs.

BlizzCon held a unique combination of business professionals, entertainment media gurus, professional e-sports players and their fans, and diehard *World of Warcraft* players. You could feel the fabrics of these colliding cultures weaving together a weird but warm quilt of flashing lights and overblown spectacle.

The first day of the event, my mom dropped me off near the convention center around 9 a.m. I picked up my badge from the check-in and people-watched for a few minutes. My anxiety about meeting Margot was briefly dulled by the crowd of Warcraft cosplayers, fans sporting their faction's t-shirt, dudes in sweatshirts embroidered with their class patches, and people holding up signs with their avatar's name written on them for potential in-game friends to spot. These were my people. Everyone was so damn nice to each other.

I arrived on the floor of Margot's hotel room practically breathless, as if I had sprinted up a flight of stairs to meet her. I stood in front of her hotel room door with my jaw clenched, heart racing, and a nervous recognition that this was the first time I'd be around a girl who liked me.

She swung the door open, I flashed a big dumb smile at her, and we hugged. I was relieved to find that Margot was shorter than me. We started talking at bullet-speed about rumors of the upcoming expansion pack, *Wrath of the Lich King*, which was supposedly going to be announced at BlizzCon later that day. The more we talked about the thing we mutually loved, the more my self-doubt melted away.

Margot and I met with the rest of our guildies in front of the convention center, embracing each other and chatting excitedly. Most of us already had a general idea of what the others looked like from posting pictures of ourselves on our guild forums. At some point in the meeting, each one of us was told, "You are exactly how I imagined you'd be!"

We roved into the convention center, thirteen of us guildies, a tight-knit group of friends who had known each other for three years yet were meeting for the first time. The group was inseparable, taking measures not to lose a single person in the thick of the BlizzCon crowd. The same cohesion that was demanded of our team online had carried over into our real-world dynamic, and it was a beautiful thing.

The opening ceremonies of BlizzCon began. My guild had claimed an entire row near the front and center of the auditorium. Chris Metzen, the lead designer and narrative godfather of the entire Warcraft series, made his way onstage to announce the forthcoming expansion of *World of Warcraft*. When the cinematic for *Wrath of the Lich King* began, the entire audience erupted into applause. *WoW* players had been jonesing for a narrative conclusion to *Warcraft III*'s *The Frozen Throne* expansion after its foreboding ending depicted the Lich King scaling the icy pinnacle of Northrend's frozen throne. The expansion offered that and more.

The rest of the weekend was spent walking the floor of the convention center, playing demos of the upcoming expansion, testing out *Diablo III* and *StarCraft 2*, and going to late-night hotel parties. I drank alcohol for the first time during an excursion into the ballroom of a Hyatt, sipping a rum and coke with reckless teenage abandon.

Throughout the weekend, Margot and I stole away to take walks around the convention center, talking about what we were most excited about in the upcoming expansion, what we couldn't stand about our high schools, and what we planned to do after graduation. I knew I wanted to make video games, I just didn't know how I'd do it. She knew she wanted to move to the United States, she just didn't know how she'd do it.

I jokingly told her that I'd marry her so that she could get citizenship. She joked about the audit into our relationship, that the Bureau of Citizenship would see logs and logs of chat exchanges via *World of Warcraft* and deem our relationship an absurd fantasy set up purely for the visa.

Despite my guildies' intentions of playing a lot of *WoW* in-person during BlizzCon, we never got around to it. The majority of our time was spent shooting the shit in our hotel rooms, sipping at pocket-sized mini-bar bottles of booze and nerding out about what we would do *later* in the game's upcoming expansion.

BlizzCon ended. Margot gave me a peck of a kiss before my mom came and picked me up in front of the Radisson. She was back on a plane for the UK later that morning, and our relationship returned to private messages via *World of Warcraft* and routine phone calls.

That weekend was more energizing than a druid's Invigorate spell. The person I was crushing on online met me in person and, despite my crushing anxiety leading up to the meet, really dug me back. My doubts about myself weren't given a leg to stand on, and I began to feel hints at a newfound confidence in talking to girls outside of *World of Warcraft*.

Six months later, Margot graduated high school and quit playing *World of Warcraft*, and I never saw or heard from her again.

On That Happy Note, Let's Talk About Divorce

Now that we've covered the dating pool that is Azeroth, let's talk about the opposite effect playing *World of Warcraft* has on existing relationships: extremely high divorce rates.

On January 31, 2012, user Lokien began a discussion thread called "*World of Warcraft* and Divorce" on *WoW*'s public forums,

So, Im just curious how many people out there have a wife or a husband who does not play this game and give them a hard time for playing? How many people have gotten the dreaded divorce because of the game or in some way related to it?

I wanna hear some tips to help a married couple stay married and not let a game ruin their relationship! Ill Start..

To keep my wife off my meat grinder what I say is "Hun, I will do the dishes tonight as long as I can play Warcraft a extra hour" That usually works.

Or more simplistic I say "Hey babe you haven't visited your mom in awhile, Why don't you go see her?"

And if those don't work I just wait until she passes out for bed and I hop on till 2am Who cares if your tired for work?

I hope that Lokien was successful in keeping his wife off of his meat grinder, but the statistics are not in his favor. When someone refuses quality time with their spouse in favor of raiding and chilling with guildies, it does not improve the health of the marriage.

A study performed by Divorce Online in 2011 found that of the wives who cite "unreasonable behavior" for ending their marriage, 15% believe their partners put gaming before them. That is a 10% increase from a similar study done in 2005, when they found that same justification only accounting for 5% of divorces. *World of Warcraft* has been named the prime culprit behind this staggering statistic, followed by the Call of Duty series in a close second.

Typically, a marriage begins to deteriorate when a spouse notices that their partner's online gaming activity has become an addiction, taking precedent over all other duties and relationships. Despite numerous appeals from the spouse, the excessive gaming is not mitigated and the partner's requests are dismissed.

There seem to be two ways a *WoW* player can solve this problem. The first is to take your spouse's complaint as a wake-up call and heavily cut back on your gaming. The second—as Earthweaver, a level 100 Tauren Shaman on Lokien's thread suggests—is a bit sneakier:

> I introduced my wife to the game. Set her up with hunter (You get pets!!). Helped her learn to play and hand held through some leveling.
>
> She is now just as addicted as I am.
> Problem Solved.

Earthweaver may be an enabler, but he has clued in on something real. In 2012, researchers from Brigham Young University published a study of 349 couples evaluating the impact of MMORPGs such as *World of Warcraft* on their marital satisfaction. They found that 76% of married couples where both spouses play found that gaming had a positive effect on their marriage. Inversely, 75% of couples where only one spouse played reported that their partner's gaming habits were a significant source of unhappiness in the marriage.

So to save your marriage you can either rope your partner into slaying epic dragons with you and become the next Azerothian power couple, or you can cut back on gaming and reinvest in your IRL marriage. After all, it is perhaps worth listening to your partner's concern. They understand you, they care about you, and they may remember a time when you had aspirations outside the vortex of infinite online escape.

Or, as Lokien so charmingly suggests, I am pained to report that there is a third option:

Blizzard should sell Spouse cages on their website.
So whenever you want to play just lock them up.

Yes, totally. Thank you, Lokien.

PART 4:
GRIEFERS, TROLLS,
AND OTHER MONSTERS

Tribes of Warcraft

WHEN PLAYING AS ONE of my alternate characters, a female Tauren Druid, I joined a pick-up group of assembled strangers to attempt a dungeon. I was the group's main healer, and I did my job on autopilot. The content wasn't demanding, and we all appeared to know the dungeon's encounters well. When the tank piled on more enemies than he could chew, our party wiped, and the group leader called me "a dumb fucking bitch" and told me "this is why chix cant play WOW!!!" before removing me from the group.

I was a tourist in the land of misogyny. Actual women live there.

To get a better perspective on harassment in *WoW*'s culture, I spoke with Devony Schmidt, a former guildmate of mine with whom I've maintained a real-life friendship post-*WoW*. "I'd have people in parties of course make jokes like 'tits or gtfo' if I made a comment that indicated I was female," Schmidt told me, "or there was a lot of 'women don't exist on the internet' kind of stuff, and general surprise if I talked on Ventrilo [...] The biggest type of targeting was that I would often get offered 'gifts' by male players (one of which later harassed me for nude photos)."

As in all places on the internet, anonymity in *WoW* breeds aggressive behavior, which tends to be directed toward often-marginalized groups of people. *World of Warcraft's* player base frequently displays downright despicable acts of racism and sexism in both public forums and private messages. *WoW* players often engage in trolling, a form of internet abuse in which a player makes it their personal mission to make other players' experiences in the game a living hell.

In an article titled "Guild Life in the *World of Warcraft*: Online Gaming Tribalism," Thomas Brignall writes,

> Virtual worlds are not free from real-world stereotypes and prejudices. Stereotypes and cultural identities follow players into the game. Anonymity allows individuals to avoid the negative consequences of being prejudicial to other players. According to Blizzard Entertainment's rules on its website, the company enforces policies that forbid prejudicial language. Blizzard Entertainment has not published how frequently it enforces this rule. In a world where individuals can behave as they choose, and avoid people they dislike, hard-core players often employed tribalistic techniques in order to associate only with players they liked. Some groups displayed high

levels of unity and cooperation. However, there were frequent occurrences of groups fragmenting into smaller subgroups. When our guild's population fragmented into smaller isolated groups, competition and resentment ensued.

Enter the griefer, such a frequent occurrence in our online gaming culture that it warrants its own Wikipedia article, which defines it as "a player in a multiplayer video game who deliberately irritates and harasses other players within the game, using aspects of the game in unintended ways. A griefer derives pleasure primarily or exclusively from the act of annoying other users, and as such is a particular nuisance in online gaming communities, since griefers often cannot be deterred by penalties related to in-game goals."

Let's chew on how sad this description is: A griefer *derives pleasure primarily or exclusively from the act of annoying other users.*

I fear that my younger self would have been fully indoctrinated into the world of the griefer were it not for the fact that I initially started playing *World of Warcraft* with my stepdad. Had I been left unmonitored, free to roam the digital playground on my own, I am certain that I would have been tempted by the surrounding harsh culture and devolved into the lowest of all internet lowlifes.

I lived by a similar logic in real life: I'd get bullied by popular kids that I perceived as cool, so in return I tried to bully kids to earn the same kind of "coolness" that I thought my tormentors had received from picking on me. Perpetuating this cycle of projected internal pain, of course, did not make me any cooler or feel any better.

Even with my stepdad's influence, I pulled some shady moves when I first began playing *WoW*. I would send obnoxious in-game messages to players asking for handouts of gold or items, I'd attempt to ninja-loot items off of bosses (stealing an item off of a defeated enemy before the rest of the group can place their bid for the desired item), and I'd throw a tantrum if I was killed by another player out in the field or lost a piece of loot to another player.

One evening shortly after I began playing *WoW*, Joe and I—from our two computers under the same roof—were questing with a small group others when I lost a rare item in a random lottery to another player. I flipped out on the group—made a big scene about it. The player had won the item fairly, but *I wanted it*. Soon I heard a knock at my bedroom door and Joe popped his head in to tell me, "Hey, you know you're being kind of a dick."

In my thirteen years, adults had called me a brat, obnoxious, rude—"dick" was a new one. I was supremely oblivious to why I was being called a dick, and thankfully my stepdad was patient enough to explain to me how my behavior toward random people on this game meant I was developing an aggressive, unpleasant persona. He told me he didn't find it enjoyable to be around. I was being a dick. I never griefed again.

Block and Get Over It

What improved my online etiquette even further was joining my raiding guild, which to this day helped shape how I handle online interpersonal relationships. Perhaps even all of my relationships. Tolerance for jerks, like in real life, was pretty low. Our guild actively purged trolls, and the barrier of entry to our social circle came so high that we didn't experience much trouble. The ability to block anyone who you do not get along with at the push of a button remains a remarkable tool of online social activity.

The "Block List" combined with guild formation has created what Thomas Brignall calls "online gaming tribalism." Brignall argues that online communities and guilds are not simply alternate realities, but entirely new social identities. These communities offer unification for people who identify with one another under a system that can immediately banish anyone who goes against the grain of the group's shared ideology.

Though the guild culture that I've written about thus far has been the hardcore raiding guild, it is not the only kind of guild that has formed within *World of Warcraft*. More common than raiding guilds are social guilds, which formed purely to have a group of people to consistently chat with. A social guild could be exclusive to certain ethnicities, religions, ages, or geographical locations. If there was a tribe you identified with in the world, chances were you could find it in *WoW*. And, if you wished, you could easily block out everything else.

While blocking and grouping off may be necessary, its ease can be a problem. Brignall notes that tribalism "detracts from the unity of the general population. Further, because of the breakdown of the general population into smaller, more isolated groups, tribalism frequently creates inner struggles, competition, and an us versus them mentality within a civilized society. Eventually, various tribes within the social structure become openly hostile toward other tribes."

So what does Blizzard do when a guild cultivates an internal culture in favor of griefing, or even beyond griefing and into the realm of flat-out hate speech? The short answer is nothing. Players can report other players who are harassing them on an individual basis, but the lines get a bit more blurred if they are happening inside of a guild setting.

Here is an example of a player who attempted to report the sexist and racist behaviors of a guild with a moderator from a Blizzard Customer Support forum board post made in 2013:

Player: A guild I am in is sexually harassing people on my realm and promoting racism in guild chat. I won't repeat what they've said here... It is my hope with this thread that the guild will be investigated as a whole on a more thorough level for sexual harassment and racism since I am unable to let GMs know in-game and am only able to report on a line-by-line basis.

Thank you for your time, and I am sorry this kinda of thing is so cultivated in a guild on my server =/.

Edit: I should mention I won't be leaving this guild. I want to be able to report them as much as often until something has been recorded/done so I can better protect the community I am a part of on my server. It's a good community and doesn't deserve this level of vileness.

Moderator: This is an issue.

Guilds are an at-will collection of individuals. What is said in guild chat has MUCH more lenience than what is said in public—or in whispers.

If your intention of staying in this guild is to report them, your heart is in the right place, but it's not going to be terribly fruitful unless you are reporting whispers to you.

Of course that kind of behavior is not welcome, or tolerated, if it is reported by the person receiving the communication—but THEY need to be the ones reporting. We look at such reports on a character basis, not a guild basis.

I'd normally recommend that you have a chat with your Guild Leader, but it sounds like in that guild this is tolerated and it may not get you very far.

While it makes sense that *World of Warcraft* GMs (Game Masters, in-game moderators that uphold Warcraft's terms of service) wouldn't intervene on internal guild affairs, it brings up a question of how these guild-endorsed mindsets could potentially perpetuate harmful behaviors in the *WoW* community.

This type of moderator response is apparent from Brignall's research, where he points out a systemic flaw in *World of Warcraft* that breeds negative behaviors amongst entire communities: a lack of repercussions and personal responsibility. A player under the internet's cloak of anonymity can harass another player without any personal stake and with minimal (if any) in-game repercussions. Harassment has become an acceptable part of the game. Brignall writes:

> Prejudicial conversations were commonplace in *WoW*. Some players talked about "raping female enemy characters," or emulated sex with the corpses of dead female enemies. Frequently the chat channels were teeming with racist comments. There also seemed to be a propensity for quick judgments. Frequently, Horde players perpetuated the myth that most Alliance members were teenage jocks, griefers, and unintelligent. While many players told me 'it is just a game,' the conversations about rival faction players frequently were hostile and extremely personal.

The question remains whether it is Blizzard's responsibility to curate *WoW*'s social environment. The players are given the responsibility of choosing with whom to interact. The players are the ones responsible for typing a block command to avoid a harasser's hateful messages. You can report the harassing statements that trickled through before blocking and GMs will take whatever measures they deem appropriate, but the victim will typically never learn what justice has been dealt.

Griefers could make additional characters and briefly circumvent the block option, sending additional messages to their target before receiving an additional block. This type of behavior typically resulted in a temporary account ban.

The *WoW* community's general mindset about online harassment when I was active was: Don't whine to the GM's about it. Block any offensive parties and move along. There often seemed to be an air of indifference about any abuses in the *WoW* community. It was often mused that the world is a huge place and *World of Warcraft* is a huge game, and so naturally countless assholes would pop up and make themselves known behind the guise of the internet. What could you do?

But when talking about this course of action with my guildmates, particularly the female players, many were tired of the "block and get over it" mentality. "It's always been common to see/hear racial and sexual slurs thrown around," Devony Schmidt told me, "and any suggestion that people shouldn't say things like that is immediately written off as someone being 'butthurt.'"

The female players in my guild said that they received overtly sexual messages from trolls and other players they had brief gameplay encounters with on an almost daily basis. The window between receiving these messages and the messages getting blocked still left a nasty invasive taste on the day's gaming experience. The "block and get over it" mindset reflects a larger "deal with it" culture around sexual abuse and harassment that lets women know the abuses they've faced will not be met with action or even sympathy.

When I asked Schmidt whether she'd had to frequently block players in *WoW*, she replied that she had, but that strangers were not the full extent of the problem. "It also became fairly common for people I thought of as friends to attempt to have conversations with me that were openly sexual in nature," she told me, "which was somewhat more insidious. Easier to block a random internet troll than to block someone you've actually developed a friendship with, but when they won't stop talking about how sexy your voice is and how much they miss you when you don't log on... Gets old pretty quickly, especially when all you're trying to do is log in to check your mailbox for ten seconds."

I asked Schmidt if she believed Blizzard Entertainment should take up the mantle of responsibility in cleaning up the environment they created. "I think the hard thing about a situation like this is that it's the players that have driven the creation of this culture," she replied, "and for it to have any meaningful effect, it'll almost certainly have to be the players who critique and condemn it. If it comes from above, in the form of banning, censoring, etc., it's going to make people more vehement, and honestly they'll probably just find someone (probably a woman) in the bureaucratic structure of Blizzard to blame for it—the culture will continue. [...] The change has to come from within, and it's got to naturally create the kind of community that doesn't actually isolate players. I do think developer apathy encourages this kind of environment—if Blizzard does nothing, well, the internal moderation system won't ever kick in. But I think the approach of top-down censorship won't work either."

The Judgment of the Tribunal

Perhaps it isn't the online social platform's obligation to moderate or censor its community in order to maintain a safe environment, but rather it's their responsibility to teach users what it means to conduct themselves properly.

Riot Games, the developers of *League of Legends*, a multiplayer online battle arena game (or MOBA) that in 2014 boasted 67 million players a month, noted in *LoL*'s early days that a significant number of players had quit the game citing the "noxious behavior" of other players.

In response, Riot assembled their "player behavior team," a group of Riot staff members that included PhDs in psychology, cognitive science, and neuroscience, to tackle the issue of their toxic player base.

The team began with some small reforms to *LoL*'s design. The first step was shifting how the chat system operates. Originally, players could send messages to their own teammates and to their opponents. This often led to volatile exchanges between opposing teams. Players reported that around 80% of the chat exchanges at this time were negative.

All Riot had to do was switch off chat between teams as a default option. A week after switching the default, negative chat reportedly decreased by 32.7% and positive chat increased by 34,5%. Players can still go into their settings and switch chat between teams back on, but the extra steps it takes to do that appears to be enough to quell whatever shitty message you were about to send.

Another step Riot took was to begin telling banned players, in detail, why they've been banned. This is a problem that I saw go unaddressed in *World of Warcraft*—players in *WoW* receive general warnings without any specifics. *League of Legends* now details where you went wrong and why it was wrong. Riot noted a significant decrease in players who have been banned once becoming repeat offenders.

The third and most ominous-sounding implementation Riot's behavioral team made was "The Tribunal." The Tribunal is a democratic disciplinary committee made of volunteer *LoL* players that votes on reported instances of bad behavior.

The most dramatic result of the new Tribunal system was the banning of Christian "IWillDominate" Rivera of Team Liquid, a globally recognized professional e-sports team. Pros like Rivera build their entire careers on their ability to play *League of Legends*, with salaries that can exceed six figures a year.

LoL employs an internal "harassment score" within the game to gauge a player's behavior, helping build the aforementioned psychological profiles that the behavioral team at Riot uses to evaluate their player base. Rivera ranked among the worst 0.7% of all North American players. This placed Rivera, despite his pro status, in front of a Tribunal. The final verdict in his ruling, which was approved by the case auditors at Riot, is as follows:

> His persistent tendency to engage in verbal abuse and insults, his lack of cordial demeanor, and his treatment of less-skilled players is unacceptable for any player, especially a high-profile

professional player who has a regular opportunity to lead the community by example.

On December 24, 2012, all of Rivera's accounts were banned from *LoL* due to his toxic behavior, and he was subsequently suspended from the League Championship Series for one year.

The ban on Rivera has since been lifted, and he is allowed to participate in the League Championship Series once again. In 2013, Riot offered Rivera a roadmap to earn back his LCS eligibility, and he took the opportunity, stating, "There were a series of events that transpired leading up to my restriction [from the] LCS, and for me personally it took Riot's interjection for me to realize that I could be a positive influence—not just in league but just with everything. When my mindset shifted—I started to enjoy the game more, this time not at anyone's expense."

The Tribunal system opens up a dialogue between the community of players and the developers themselves to help educate offending players about where they went wrong. It gives the harassed a voice to explain why they were offended, and it allows the developers to point out what constitutes volatile behavior. It isn't engineered to punish and banish players, but rather to rehabilitate them and build empathy in their online community. More than 280,000 players went from "censured" statues in *League of Legends* to "good standing" after the Tribunal was implemented.

The success of the Tribunal system underscores a lack of communication and accountability in MMORPGs like *World of Warcraft*. We've grown apathetic and desensitized toward outrageous behavior under the magnitude of trolls and griefers. Harassment is to be expected, and that's the problem. When we open up the lines of communication between parties, an important dialogue takes place that could never happen in the wake of a block or a ban.

PART 5:
MORE THAN OUR AVATARS

The Quest Begins

THE PINNACLE OF MY *WoW* career was from the beginning of 2007 to the middle of 2008. In this stage, I was playing roughly 40 hours a week, spending the weekends of my sophomore year and most of my junior year of high school almost exclusively in Azeroth. Understandably, my excess gaming put the spotlight of my parents' concern right on me.

Limitations were put in place: No logging on during the school week, two hours total on the weekends. I found these rules to be impossible and immediately made plans to circumvent them.

I started going to internet cafés, spending a suspicious number of hours away from home. And when that didn't work, I'd go to a friend's house and play on a computer already loaded up with *WoW*. I justified these deceptions to myself by saying that my parents could hardly understand what this guild meant to me, and that my stinted playtime would reflect poorly on me in the eyes of my guildies. But finding enablers was way more challenging in real life than it was in the game world.

The breaking point was when I attempted to install *World of Warcraft* on school PCs using a proxy server to bypass the administration's list of blocked activities.

I was caught almost immediately and reported to my parents. This resulted in a three-week grounding and complete suspension from online activities.

Still, I pride myself on my goal-oriented mind. When I focus on a task, I will drill away at it until I am satisfied, even if it's at the sacrifice of my own rest or mental stability. When I was under my parents' heavy restrictions, this creative energy was put toward finding ways to play *World of Warcraft*. I soon found the best way yet.

My guildies were coordinating a post-BlizzCon real-life meetup at one of the guild officers' homes in Phoenix, Arizona. The goal was to set up all of our computers in the living room, spend the weekend playing *WoW* together, drink, be merry, and maybe chill by the pool if we made it outside. I had never felt, nor will I ever again feel, such a necessary urge to go to Phoenix, Arizona.

The real-life guild meeting was happening the second weekend into my grounding period. I knew my parents wouldn't allow me, still a fifteen-year-old kid, to travel to the desert to meet up with a bunch of strangers I'd met online. Though the majority of my guildmates were around the age of eighteen, there were some folks in their early twenties joining us, and there was no telling what these people might be like in real life. I decided to use my internet probation to my advantage.

I concocted the story of a friend's camping trip, a trip that was actually happening, in Kern Valley. I convinced my friend to inform my parents of the logistics of the event, and my parents, perhaps blinded by surprise and a burning desire to see me engage in an outdoor activity, allowed me to go.

Beneath the subterfuge, I made plans with my two closest guildmates, two Californian fellas who were road-tripping to Arizona for the guild meeting. They agreed to swing by Irvine to pick me up. That morning I left home with my backpack and sleeping bag in tow, feeling like I had pulled off the world's greatest heist. My "camping buddy" picked me up in his parents' car, told my folks that I would be well-looked after, and then he turned the corner and stopped the car.

I snuck back behind my parent's house to my bedroom window where my computer tower was waiting for me. Before leaving, I'd bagged all of the cables and duct-taped a towel around my computer, then gently lowered the rig a foot beneath my window, expertly maneuvering what would have been an impossible object to sneak out the front door. From there, my accomplice friend dropped me off five miles away at a rendezvous point, an outdoor mall where my *World of Warcraft* buddies later retrieved me.

This was my first time meeting Austin and Andy in person. They both greeted me with a hug. The nuances and quirks of our personalities that we knew so well in each other online translated perfectly in real life. We each knew the others better than we did classmates who we saw every day. We had been playing the game together for two years at this point.

We moved a lot when I was a kid because of my mother's work. I lived in four different cities during elementary, middle, and high school. The relationships I made at each school flittered away as soon as I relocated to another city. The longest-lasting IRL friendship I had was only a year old. Although I was meeting them for the first time, Austin and Andy were my oldest friends. Hopping in that van and taking off for Arizona was one of the most liberating feelings I'd ever had.

The Fellowship Gathers

Before heading to Arizona, we had to stop in Palm Springs to pick up our guild's Warlock. We hit the road on our surreal adventure, three people who'd just met each other for the first time driving cross-country to hang out with a bunch of strangers we'd known for years.

During the six-hour drive to Palm Springs, I daringly smoked a cigarette and then drove the car, two things I had never done before. I then drove the car *while* daringly smoking a cigarette. This was what I fantasized being an adult must feel like. I imagined that you turn eighteen, a switch flips, and suddenly you're free to do whatever you want without any inhibitions. I felt a fantastical form of adulthood only possible before real adulthood.

We arrived in Palm Springs at sundown. Chris the Warlock greeted us with daft excitement when we knocked on his apartment door. Here was another man who was the spitting image of his online persona, another friend I instantly bonded with after two years of online companionship.

"Is that your rig?" I asked, pointing to a solid black foot-long rectangle trimmed with purple LED lights. "Sure is," he said. That night in lieu of resting, we played *World of Warcraft*. The four of us hopped on to our guild's Ventrilo server, finding that other guildmates were also converging on their way to Phoenix. All of my friends would soon be together, and I would be right there with them.

As the sun started to rise over Palm Springs, we each struck up a cigar. There was an exhausted lull in conversation as we puffed on smoke. I felt more socially validated from this 24-hour period than I had felt in my entire life. It was unreal. I thought about how I had run away from home to experience this. I was surprised at myself for taking such dramatic measures, and I was equally surprised by the lack of anxiety or guilt I felt.

We all got a couple of hours sleep before stopping at a Ruby's Diner in downtown Palm Springs. The four of us loaded into Andy's hippie van along with our computers and weekend backpacks. We cruised through the seven-hour ride to Phoenix, talking about *World of Warcraft*, school, aspirations, and where we wanted to be in a couple of small but infinitely distant years.

I remember my mother calling me when we were halfway to Phoenix. My throat sank into my stomach when I picked up, brewing up a swift excuse about cell phone reception being faulty between the cavernous rocky maw of Kern Valley. She asked a few questions about how the trip was going so far, and I responded with some fines and greats, trying to keep the invasive presence of my parents out of my sojourn. I hung up, Austin called me a sly motherfucker, and nothing else about my parents was brought up for the rest of the trip.

We arrived at a small apartment complex in Phoenix in the early afternoon that Saturday, greeted by several guildmates I had previously met at BlizzCon a few months prior. The spacious living room had the furniture arranged to accommodate all of the PC towers that were brought along for the journey. People were eating snacks, drinking, and chatting with each other from their computers, *World of Warcraft* running nonstop on each monitor.

Conversation hardly left the game world, seldom taking a personal turn. When we talked about our lives, we generally talked about the obligations that took us away from *World of Warcraft* before shifting back into discussions about raids, the state of the game, and what we hoped to achieve as a guild the following summer.

The weekend was spent enjoying Phoenix's early spring weather by the pool, with temperatures staying a steady 90° Fahrenheit with enough humidity to fill a water park.

When the living room-turned-computer lab got too hot and stuffy, we'd spend some time offline chatting about *WoW*, and when it came time for meals we'd all move out in one large, hungry raiding party to the nearest restaurant.

The last night we all went to a bowling alley. I discovered that gin and tonics glowed blue underneath a black light. The entire group's inside jokes, references, and history were exclusively based in *World of Warcraft*. We talked at length about events that had happened to us in-game, about how insane the anti-gravity portion of Kael'thas Sunstrider's boss fight was, how stoked we were to enter the Sunwell raid for the first time, reminiscing on these events so lucidly that it sounded as if we were personally there.

Our guild's *World of Warcraft* stories contained much more meaning than the game itself. They all pertained to what we had done together: something funny someone did during a raid, embarrassing gossip overheard in chat, or momentous triumphs we had made as one cohesive unit. We regaled ourselves with tales of our illustrious careers together in Azeroth. These were stories steeped in personality and emotion, evoking deep sentiment from the group.

What else would we talk about outside of what we knew about each other already? I didn't want to discuss the details of my stagnant high school life, or the fact that I was grounded at home and couldn't even play *WoW* without sneaking around.

No, instead I was going to talk with my friends about my badass rogue, the one who tops DPS charts and has a ton of excellent narratives about storming enemy cities. The time we killed Onyxia the Black Dragon for the first time and staked her giant scaly head in the middle of Orgrimmar for all to witness. The time our mage attended a raid a little too drunk and accidentally killed herself by falling down a large elevator shaft in Serpentshire Cavern. These were our stories, our history.

I finished the half of a gin and tonic my friend let me steal sips off of, relishing the bounty of company. I felt sad that the weekend was coming to an end, wished that all of these people lived closer to me. I pulled out my phone for the first time since arriving in Phoenix to see: "Mom (12 missed calls)."

The Quest Imperiled

"Did you know that your computer is gone?" was the first thing she asked me. I'd sprinted out of the bowling alley as soon as I saw that my mother had been repeatedly trying to get a hold of me since earlier that afternoon. "Yes," I said, "uh, I fucked something up and took it to get repaired." It was the best half-baked excuse that my gin-induced brain could concoct.

Pacing around a florescent-lit parking lot in Phoenix trying to convince my mother was not how I wanted this trip to end. She asked me how my camping trip was going, and I told her that it's been wonderful. I caught some bass in the river. I even gutted them myself after Brian's dad taught me how. We cooked them over an open fire and ate them for dinner. It was a hoot.

Any perceived suspicion I picked up in her voice disarmed and I felt the grip in my gut relieving a bit. We said our I love you's then hung up. I stood out there for a while longer, a little wobbly, before returning to my group.

The next morning the three of us loaded all of our equipment and luggage back into Andy's car and said goodbye to the guild, although we were quick to point out that we'd be seeing each other later that evening online anyway. The drive back was sleepy and uneventful, all of us tapped out from marathoning *WoW* and hanging with our online-turned-real-life pals instead of sleeping.

I got nervous upon returning to Irvine. This whole plan wasn't fulfilled to its end just yet, and I could still get caught in the act. I was dropped off a few sleepy streets away from my house, picking a low-traffic spot to avoid potential detection. I dropped my towel-wrapped computer back by my bedroom window before circling back around the house to let myself back in.

I swung the door open, was greeted by my mom and stepdad, chatted lightly about the trip, retold the fish-gutting story to my stepdad, unloaded my backpack and sleeping bag, then hopped in the shower.

I'd somehow pulled it off. I'd gotten away with it.

In fact, my parents had no clue about the stunt until I started writing this book. I called my mom and spilled the beans about the entire operation, everything from the dummy camping trip to the booze and cigarettes, and that I thought she had almost sniffed me out when she called about my computer.

Her first reaction was, "That's horrible, Daniel. That's awful. This is awful. You were a minor! You could've been killed!" And she's not wrong. It was a shitty thing to do to a parent. Despite having met our host months before at BlizzCon, this mostly adult group could have harbored anyone. To a mom, this trip was a nightmare.

I asked what she would have done if she had caught me, and she said without hesitation that she would have flown to Phoenix, whooped my ass, and taken me back home. I told her that, yeah, if my child did something like this, I'd be a nervous wreck too.

"Do you at least feel *guilty?*" my mom wanted to know.

I couldn't say that I did. This road trip was a highlight of my high school career. It was stupid, but I cherish the memory of it.

My mother would like to add that she's incredibly embarrassed that this story is included here. Thank you, Mom, for being a good sport about it all of these years later.

PART 6:
WHAT KEEPS US
COMING BACK

Variable Ratio Enforcement

CREATION REQUIRES INTENTION. BE it in fine art, a piece of software, or ad-churning clickbait, understanding work's purpose bridges the gap between the abstract and the concrete. When you set out to create a new game, it is important to ask what the game is, how it plays, what the player will spend their time doing, and what you want to convey to the player. You must ask, "Why should this game exist?" Do you want to entertain the player with nifty and innovate mechanics? To educate the player with an impactful message? To enthrall the player with a well-delivered narrative? Maybe the goal is simply to hook users into making impulsive in-app purchases, or to retain users in an MMO to keep that subscription revenue stream a-flowin'.

Jonathan Blow, the creator of the critically acclaimed games *Braid* and *The Witness*, is an outspoken critic on the state of the games industry, the potential direction of video games, and the steps we must take as game designers for the medium to reach its full potential. In a 2007 lecture at the Montreal International Games Summit titled "Design Reboot," Blow answers the big question: What are games?

"Games are trying to achieve a goal," he says, "and there are rules governing the actions. There are effects on what you can do in the world and what the worlds can [do] back. Games create a low-stakes subdomain that create a 'meaning of life'... you know why you're there, and you know what you're trying to do." For Blow, realizing how much a game's "meaning of life" was wrapped up in its gameplay fundamentally changed how he approached game creation.

Blow's concept can be expressed in a similar, albeit more technical way, as the "gameplay loop." A game's gameplay loops are its possible mechanics. Though there's no limit to what can comprise a loop, and a game can contain many loops at once. For example, *Super Mario Bros.*'s most basic gameplay loop might look like:

Run right → smoosh bad guys underfoot → smash blocks → reach the level's end → repeat

Whereas a loop from a Final Fantasy game might look like:

Advance the plot → level up → find loot → repeat

And a Mass Effect game's loop might look like:

Advance the plot → level up → find loot →
GET DOWN WITH SOME FINE SPACE
HOTTIES, DAYUUUUUM → make some
plot/character choices → repeat

For game creators, being able to articulate your game's gameplay loops helps to focus your attention on what matters. When you are considering adding new mechanics, you can ask, "How will this mechanic improve, complicate, or otherwise impact the game's loop?" After all, the aspect of the game that matters most is whatever the player is spending the most time doing.

For example, in *Half-Life 2* you spend most of your time shooting future alien Gestapo baddies with various guns—therefore, the game is primarily a first-person shooter. This much is obvious. But what makes *Half-Life 2* such a successful first-person shooter is that the developers paid so much attention to making the primary gameplay loop as interesting, innovative, and *fun* as possible. They asked themselves, "What will keep the action of blasting baddies from being repetitive and bland?"

While developing *Failsafe*, my studio's pilot project, we wanted to make sure that the player didn't feel like the designers were wasting their time. We didn't want to fill our loops with fluff and filler content to buffer *Failsafe's* playtime. *Failsafe* is a narrative-heavy exploration game, so we focused on making our gameplay loops emphasize those elements:

Explore → overcome environmental obstacles & puzzles → advance the plot → repeat

A game like *Failsafe* has a very clear end after its plot is resolved and its secrets are uncovered. Its business model doesn't rely on player retention. The player can enjoy it, shelve it like a nice book, and then suggest it to friends.

World of Warcraft requires a different formula. Its gameplay loop looks like:

Kill stuff → level up → get loot → repeat until endgame

Then:

Kill stuff → get loot → kill harder stuff → get better loot → repeat

The "meaning of life" in *World of Warcraft*, then, is to grow a powerful character. Defeat the endgame content and gear yourself up enough so when new, more challenging content arrives, you'll be prepared to repeat the loop. Each new patch of content scales up incrementally from the last, so that new dungeons and raids are challenging enough to necessitate that a group be geared out in the loot provided in the last patch. If a player does not keep up, they risk falling behind in their viability for newer content.

This model for an MMORPG makes sense. An MMO takes huge upfront investment as well as financial upkeep. Logically, you want to ensure that your players are good and hooked, and that their $15 a month keeps coming. I don't consider this to be a malicious tactic on behalf of game development studios to ensnare their player bases to continue generating capital.

But as Blow says in his talk, "We don't intend to harm players but we might be harming them. When tens of millions of people buy our game, we are pumping a mental substance into the mental environment—it's a public mental health issue. It's kind of scary but it's kind of cool because we have the power to shape humanity." Like any creators, we can't know all the effects our games will have on the world, yet we are at least in a small way accountable for how our games are used by players. In the case of *WoW*, Blizzard is partly responsible for how wholly the game takes over players' lives.

Games are addictive for a multitude of reasons. *Call of Duty* has a delicious mindlessness to it. *Spelunky* is masterfully challenging. *The Elder Scrolls IV: Oblivion* has a beautiful combination of exploration, gameplay, and story that kept me hooked for months. *Candy Crush* has its bright happy responsiveness and the diabolical ease of its microtransactions. *World of Warcraft* immerses players in its stylized fantasy world and combines it with the high stakes of working and competing with other real people.

Such stakes reached beyond the game's core gameplay. To remain on the cutting edge of competitive raiding, we had to make modifications to the base *WoW* game. Raiding guilds often require user interface augmentations, onscreen timers, and boss indicators to be installed by raiders to so the party could perform optimally.

For example, as a Rogue, a class whose sole purpose in *World of Warcraft* is to dish out as much hurt as possible, there was a sequence of abilities that, when executed, offered the mathematically highest output of damage possible against a boss. A Rogue during the *Wrath of the Lich King* expansion era would focus primarily on three abilities: Slice N' Dice, Rupture, and Deadly Poison. I stripped away my user interface of all of Blizzard's aesthetic flare and replaced it with a stripped-down UI that provided a minimal menu of abilities and a series of timers that would stream a ticker of timers. The meaning of my life in *World of Warcraft* was no longer to be immersed in the game's world, but to compete at the highest level possible.

In Alex Golub's article "Being in the World (of Warcraft)," a great quote from HolyHealz, raid leader of the guild Power Aeternus, encapsulates the spirit of this style of gameplay:

> Personally I really enjoy pushing the pace, challenging myself: how hard, how efficient I could be, how much I could push damage, how I could survive. That sort of thing was the first reason why I chose to raid, and that continues to be a motivating factor. Eventually it really became about when you achieve common goals, as a group you really build strong camaraderie and strong connections. When you're raiding in Molten Core and you're killing bosses for the first time and doing server firsts or close to server firsts, it was an incredible high. And the amount of people yelling on vent when we killed Ragnaros was amazing. It was like nothing has even been louder. There will always be those first kills that I remember.

I similarly remember the euphoric rush of my guild's first boss kills. The onscreen event of a boss's health hitting 0%, the ensuing screams over Ventrilo, the praise between guildmates, the distribution of loot. It was a party. This is what hardcore raiders returned to, over and over again. Not only the experience of the kill, but the reveling in it, the praise and celebration amongst your team. What a loop.

Nowadays, *World of Warcraft* doesn't offer the experiences I look for in a game. I typically stick to shorter games that either lean heavily on neat storytelling or interesting gameplay concepts. *World of Warcraft* without a raiding guild is a dull experience for me. As Jonathan Blow points out, "MMOs are notorious for having relatively empty gameplay, but keeping players hooked with constant fake rewards—this creates 'the treadmill.' Rewards are a way of lying to the player so they feel good and continue to play the game." He noted some extreme examples of this, such as reported incidents of Chinese and Korean MMO players dying at the computer. "As long as players are hooked, it doesn't matter how good the core gameplay is. As long as they want to get the nicer sword, they'll still play the game, and as long as they play it's all the same to us as designers—I'm sure at this point, people think I'm needlessly babbling on about this point. But I want to put forth this question: Would they still play a game if it took out all the scheduled rewards?"

The gameplay loops of *World of Warcraft* follow the psychological theory of "variable ratio enforcement." We know that rats, monkeys, and people work harder and longer at whatever they're doing when a reward is in place. But unlike on a fixed-ratio reward schedule, where, for example, a rat gets a food pellet every ten times it hits a lever, on a variable-ratio schedule, the reward is provided after an unpredictable number of responses. Not knowing when we will get our reward makes us hit the level/raid the dungeon all the more often.

The type of player that *World of Warcraft* creates is generally one that's hungry for this reward reinforcement. A raider is looking to fulfill that side of the gameplay loop, to receive better gear for their character, to progress further and further down the endless chain of content. The question this poses is: What does this cultivate inside of a player besides repetitive consumption? What happens when a gameplay loop never reaches an endpoint but rather traps its player inside of a whirlpool of content?

The task ahead of game developers is a challenging one. It is becoming increasingly impossible to strike a balance between creating fulfilling game experiences and meeting your bottom line. To me, though, this balance begins with allowing players to keep their gaming and their lives separate. The free-to-play model, which typically relies on the retention of its players for microtransactions, is the antithesis to this idea.

As *World of Warcraft*'s player base shrinks, MMO-RPGs have the potential to cultivate healthier behaviors, the way *Minecraft* encourages its players to explore the depths of their own creativity within the gamespace.

That, or we'll keep seeing more of the same proven business model based on products that profit from our unhealthy tendencies. If there is to be a break in the cycle, it will be up to the players to decide what they find worthy of their time and money.

Silver Lining

I was convinced that I wanted to make video games when I was four years old. I remember my friend Kyle booting up his Nintendo 64 loaded with *Super Mario 64*. A giant mustachioed head appeared, and I spent half an hour pointing a gloved hand around, grabbing at its cheeks, nose, chin, eyelids, all before my friend told me to actually play the game. *What, I'm not already?*

I didn't know what form my desire to make games would take, or how to begin learning the basic workflows to create games, but I immersed myself in gaming culture. G4 TV, in the days before it merged with TechTV and began airing four-hour blocks of *COPS* reruns, started airing a show called *The Electric Playground. EP* visited video game development studios, toured their nerd-haven campuses, and interviewed developers like Peter Molyneux (creator of *Populous*,

Dungeon Keeper, and *Black & White*), John Romero (who designed *Wolfenstein 3D, Doom, Quake*), and John Carmack (who programmed all three games). It was a window into a world I wanted to be a part of.

I soon became obsessed with the culture of game development. I wanted to know the people making the games, to see where they worked, and to learn the minutiae of what they did all day. When I found that Blizzard Entertainment was headquartered in my hometown of Irvine, California, working for Blizzard became the focal point in my fantasy of a career in game development. Blizzard often held creative competitions in art and design, and invited the talented young winners to their campus, so I began to work on an entry that I hoped would get their attention.

I first started practicing game design with *Neverwinter Nights*, an isometric point-and-click role-playing game derived from Dungeons & Dragons's Forgotten Realms canon. *Neverwinter* has an in-depth level creator inside of the game client that accounts for most of the game development workflows. You can design levels using every single asset and model *Neverwinter* has to offer, and you can script entirely new gameplay encounters using the LUA scripting language inside the *Neverwinter* level editor. The game had a community of independent developers who used this editor to share hours of gameplay that could be accessed through the game.

I was engrossed in *Neverwinter*'s gameplay and story. Discovering such an in-depth level editor and an entire community creating new content was incredibly inspiring. Many of the user-created levels, brimming with creativity, were nearly indistinguishable from the core content developed by Obsidian Entertainment.

I taught myself LUA scripting and adapted to the small learning curve of the level editor, and from there spent hours crafting levels to share with my friends and family. Being able to share the levels I made and watching people enjoy them was a huge pleasure, I found their feedback enormously useful at this early stage. For many people starting to make games, a lack of immediate feedback can be a barrier to digging further into game design. It can take a lot of time to get a game up and running well enough to share with people. For me, *Neverwinter*'s level editor did a good job of mitigating this problem, and my success within the level editor was what pushed me out of the *Neverwinter* sandbox into modding for other games, and then eventually into modeling tools like Autodesk Maya and game engines such as Unreal 3.

Despite any qualms I have with the empty mechanics of *World of Warcraft* or the potentially disruptive nature of its gameplay, *WoW* was the kind of game I wanted to create: a huge interactive canvas with beautiful environments and an entire culture of people sharing its world. A massive team of artists, engineers, and storytellers was working together to create a world that millions of people got to enjoy. *World of Warcraft* was the first game to make me think of games as art. I wanted in.

I met plenty of creatives inside Azeroth who'd been similarly inspired, people who made drawings, comics, fan fictions, and poems about their experiences inside the game, and animated elaborate machinima videos to create lore around their own player characters. *World of Warcraft* is such a ripe catalyst for creatives that the amount of art made inside of and about *WoW* dwarfs the actual game content.

Senior year of high school, I was able to visit Blizzard's gated Irvine campus without needing to win a competition. Through my mother I met Erin Catto, a physics programmer at Blizzard Entertainment, and geeked out to him about my various *WoW*-related passions. He was kind enough to fulfill my nerd dream and invite me to visit the campus.

Erin's work in physics programming is unparalleled. Throughout *Diablo III*, whenever you see a piece of abandoned furniture explode into a bouquet of splinters, a wall shatter into a hail of stone, or a demon flail off into a bottomless pit, that is Erin's handiwork at play.

Visiting the Blizzard campus was like my own real-life episode of Electric Playground. Inside the monolithic blue gate crowned with two-foot lettering "BLIZZARD ENTERTAINMENT" were four huge office buildings, some basketball courts, and at the center of the campus: a twelve-foot statue of an orc riding a dire wolf. Catto greeted me and we started on a tour of the grounds.

The studio's decor ran counter to how most corporate offices present themselves. There were the necessities—a front desk, meeting rooms, a water cooler—but there was also a tiki bar, video game consoles and arcade machines, bookcases filled with every computer game imaginable, and life-sized statues of beloved characters from Warcraft, Diablo, and StarCraft.

Catto walked me through a museum dedicated to Warcraft, a space that contained all of the franchise's hundreds of awards, first edition prints of the games, and some of *World of Warcraft*'s original, now-retired servers. We walked through a movie theater, an orchestral recording studio, and a state-of-the-art gym. "It's hard for people to leave sometimes," Erin joked.

We had lunch at the cafeteria and chatted about our favorite aspects of *World of Warcraft*. I was excited and a little surprised to find that many developers at Blizzard actively played *WoW* themselves: excited because it was neat knowing that the people who created *WoW* were passionate enough about it to play it, surprised because the developers were clocking in nearly as much playtime as I was.

Visiting Blizzard's campus sharpened my resolve. I wanted to make *World of Warcraft*. And if not *World of Warcraft*, games like *World of Warcraft*. Here was a huge campus of people all working toward a goal based on their shared love for video games. *WoW* was the product of their collective skill, imagination, and hard work—it benefitted from one employee's art skills, another's gift for level design, another's elegant sense of physics. Everyone had a place at this campus, and each of their unique talents shone in the game itself.

Hub Cities

Returning to *World of Warcraft* after quitting is a lot like revisiting your hometown after a long time away. The Blockbuster Video has been demolished and replaced by a Bank of America. The grove of trees you used to steal oranges from has been bulldozed for the expansion of a shopping center. All of your friends are gone. You're a stranger.

My guild began to deteriorate when three of its key leaders cut back on their hours. It started with the raid leader, who because of a new job and girlfriend, cut his raiding schedule in half. Raids became increasingly unorganized and ineffective without our leader's familiar charisma and deft ability to maneuver the group into a consolidated, powerful machine.

Our main tank started to cut down hours shortly after the raid leader did. The heavy mantle of leadership fell onto the tank's shoulders, and the difficulty and accountability of the new job was not a sustainable or desirable activity for him. With the main tank gone, our main healer also departed. The well-oiled gears lost three integral cogs, and the raiding machine ceased.

Our raid schedule was put on hiatus so the remaining guild leadership could review and recruit potential applicants, but during this time the guild lost many members to more active raiding guilds. I cut my playtime down as well. It made me anxious to log on and see my once prominent guild in such disarray. The game became less and less appealing as the deterioration persisted.

I was halfway through my junior year of high school when I decided to take a break from the game. Away from the demanding schedule of my *WoW* life, I became more active at school and my academics improved. I also got involved in theater, school politics (I became the president of both the culinary club and the game development club), and started dating. *World of Warcraft* was no longer the center of my social life.

After about a month of "taking a break" from *World of Warcraft*, I'd log on intermittently and play maybe once or twice a week for a few hours. By this time, my guild's once-bustling roster was down to me and one or two other people.

I had the opportunity to rebuild. I searched a few large raiding guilds' websites, found some openings for raiding positions I likely could have easily obtained. When entertaining the idea to apply, the years of raiding and relationship-building with my guild washed over me. Did I really want to repeat all of that again? Did I need to start that process over again?

As my playtime was winding down, I visited the old *Burning Crusade*-era hub city of Shattrath. Hub cities are the cities where the majority of the online player base congregate, where they have easy access to vendors, portals to other cities, banks, and sometimes auction houses (used to access the player-based trading economy). Each expansion of *World of Warcraft* features a new hub city of some kind, and the majority of *WoW*'s new content is generally focused around the region of the new hub city. After a new expansion takes the stage, the previous hub city becomes a ghost town. These retired hub cities evoke a vibe that is both creepy and wildly nostalgic.

My visit to Shattrath was in 2008, and the new hub city was the majestic wizard's capital of Dalaran. Shattrath's mystical enclave of curved ziggurats with crystalline peaks and enchanted gravity-defying waterfalls was abandoned. I didn't find their banks bustling with players, their taverns blossoming with conversation, or their portal rooms filled with hundreds of travelers heading to their next destination in Azeroth.

Instead I found the massive city filled with non-playable characters standing idle, stoic, fixed—eternal in their programming. My computer used to experience performance issues attempting to render the abundance of players active in Shattrath. Now it was just me, maybe one other player leveling up a new character, left alone in a vast city designed to fit multitudes of adventuring companions.

My own "hub city," my guild, was now vacated too. Our chat channels were empty, our Ventrilo servers abandoned. The person responsible for paying for our guild website canceled the subscription. Everyone had moved on, either in real life or in the game.

After walking the empty streets of Shattrath, I typed "<3" into my guild's chat tab, watched the green text fade out, and logged off. It was time for me to find a new hub city, but it would not be in *World of Warcraft*.

NOTES

What I Talk About When I Talk About Warcraft

Statistics on *World of Warcraft*'s subscribers come from Statista. com (http://bit.ly/1aA6aj9), whose data is based off public quarterly reports from Activision Blizzard. These reports are available from 2009 to the present at http://bit.ly/24VVBPd.

The Escapist

Mario Lehenbauer-Baum and Martina Fohringer's article "Towards Classification Criteria for Internet Gaming Disorder: Debunking Differences Between Addiction and High Engagement in a German Sample of World of Warcraft Players" was published in *Computers in Human Behavior*, vol. 45, April 2015.

The article "The Social Side of Gaming: How Playing Online Computer Games Creates Online and Offline Social Support" was written by the University of Hamburg's Institute of Social Psychology's Sabine Trepte, Leonard

Reinecke, Keno Juechems, and was published in *Computers in Human Behavior*, vol. 28, issue 3, May 2012.

The Design of a Hardcore Raider

Roger Caillois's book *Man, Play, and Games* was first published in English by Free Press of Glencoe in 1961, translated by Meyer Barash from the original French *Les jeux et les hommes: Le masque et le virtige* (1958).

The book *Building Successful Online Communities* was first published in 2011 by MIT Press, with Robert E. Kraut and Paul Resnick as its chief authors. The chapter "Encouraging Commitment in Online Communities" was written by Yuqing Ren, Robert E. Kraut, Sara Kiesler and Paul Resnick.

Alex Golub's article "Being in the World (of Warcraft): Raiding, Realism, and Knowledge Production in a Massively Multiplayer Online Game" was published in *Anthropological Quarterly*, vol. 83, issue 1, Winter 2010.

Exodus's guild leader Killars's public Facebook post dated April 26, 2013 may be found here: http://bit.ly/1V6UQQw

WoW player SynCaine's September 13, 2007 post "Looking in the mirror; the sickness that was WoW Raiding" may be found on his blog Hardcore Casual: http://bit.ly/1ThfY1J

Margot

Attendance figures and other data on BlizzCon were sourced from WoWWiki (http://bit.ly/1TWwC9f) and Wikipedia (http://bit.ly/1WB2Z1i), both of which do a fine job of collating this scattered information.

That study of more than 19,000 married individuals was "Marital Satisfaction and Break-ups Differ Across On-line and Off-line Meeting Venues" written by John T. Cacioppoa, Stephanie Cacioppoa, Gian C. Gonzagab, Elizabeth L. Ogburnc, and Tyler J. VanderWeelec. It was published in *Proceedings of the National Academy of Sciences* (*PNAS*), vol. 110, no. 25, June 18, 2013.

The Entertainment Software Association has published the annual report *Essential Facts About the Computer and Video Game Industry* since 2004. The reports from 2004-2009 are currently hosted at the Princeton University Library. The reports from 2010 through 2014 can be found here: http://bit.ly/1R5bXv6. The 2015 report (in PDF) can be found at http://bit.ly/1CLEhg4, and the 2016 report (also in PDF) can be found here: http://bit.ly/1XYOilD.

Newzoo's 2014 percentage of female *WoW* players was sourced from Drew Harwell's October 17, 2014 Washington Post article "More women play video games than boys, and other surprising facts lost in the mess of Gamergate," which can be found at http://wapo.st/1Ok7lS2. Newzoo's 2015 percentage of female players, as well as *WoW*'s total player number 7.1 million, comes from Saira Mueller's July 8, 2015 International Business Times article "Female WoW Players Tell All: What Is World Of Warcraft Really Like For Them?", which can be found here: http://bit.ly/1NTnwX2.

Stephanie Rosenbloom's New York Times article "It's Love at First Kill" was published on April 22, 2011, and may be found here: http://nyti.ms/1TWIlEB

On That Happy Note, Let's Talk About Divorce

Lokien's January 31, 2012 discussion thread "World of Warcraft and Divorce" (including comments by Earthweaver) may be found on Battle.net's forums: http://blizz.ly/23VEsTl

Information on the 2011 study conducted by Divorce Online was reported in both popular and gaming news sources. Information here was taken from Lydia Warren's article "Video games being blamed for divorce as men 'prefer World of Warcraft to their wives'," updated on May 31, 2011. It may be found here on DailyMail.com: http://dailym.ai/1stD13f.

Brigham Young University researchers Michelle Ahlstrom and Neil Lundberg's study of 349 couples is titled "Me, My Spouse, and My Avatar: The Relationship Between Marital Satisfaction and Playing Massively Multiplayer Online Role-Playing Games (MMORPGs)" and was published in *Journal of Leisure Research*, vol. 44, no. 1, 2012.

Tribes of Warcraft

Thomas Brignall's quotes here and elsewhere are from the chapter "Guild Life in the World of Warcraft: Online Gaming Tribalism," published in the book *Electronic Tribes* edited by Tyrone L. Adams and Stephen A. Smith, published by University of Texas Press in June 2009.

Block and Get Over It

The exchange between the *World of Warcraft* player and the Blizzard Customer Support forum moderator occured in a 2013 thread titled "Guild is Sexually Harassing / Racist." It can be found on Battle.net's forums: http://blizz.ly/1NwiBQy

The Judgment of the Tribunal

Background on Riot Games' attempt to fix *League of Legend's* online culture can be found in Michael McWhertor's October 13, 2012 article "The League of Legends team of scientists trying to cure 'toxic behavior' online: Riot Games turns to psychology to combat negativity" published at Polygon: http://bit.ly/1zR9GeY

The Tribunal ruling on *LoL* player Christian "IWillDominate" Rivera can be found on the game's official foums here: http://riot.com/1TWInMJ

Variable Ratio Enforcement

Jonathan Blow delivered his lecture "Design Reboot" at the Montreal International Games Summit on November 27, 2007. Quotes from this section were taken from Brandon Boyer and Leigh Alexander's report on the lecture, "MIGS 2007: Jonathan Blow On The 'WoW Drug', Meaningful Games," published the following day on November 28 at Gamasutra: http://ubm.io/1Xw1ccP. On November 29, Blow released the audio and slides for the lecture on the official *Braid* blog: http://bit.ly/1TUewBK

HolyHealz's quote comes from from Alex Golub's "Being in the World (of Warcraft): Raiding, Realism, and Knowledge Production in a Massively Multiplayer Online Game," cited above.

Silver Lining

John Romero and Peter Molyneux appeared in season 1, episode 1 of *The Electric Playground*, first aired on September 23, 1997 and available on YouTube at https://youtu.be/IrmBHPL5Kfc. John Carmack appeared in season 1, episode 12, first aired on December 7, 1997 and available at https://youtu.be/TfeSMaztDVc.

ACKNOWLEDGEMENTS

Thank you, Michael P. Williams, for the massive research assistance for this book.

Thank you, Gabe Durham, for being a stellar editor and publisher.

Thank you, Brian Hewes, for letting me read bits of this book at you for the last year.

Thank you, Devony Schmidt, the smartest person on the planet, for taking time to speak with me about our time shared in *World of Warcraft*.

Thank you, Austin and Andy, wherever y'all are in the world today.

Thank you, old guildies, for your community.

Thanks, Mom.

SPECIAL THANKS

For making our second season of books possible, Boss Fight Books would like to thank Ken Durham, Jakub Koziol, Cathy Durham, Maxwell Neely-Cohen, Adrian Purser, Kevin John Harty, Gustav Wedholm, Theodore Fox, Anders Ekermo, Jim Fasoline, Mohammed Taher, Joe Murray, Ethan Storeng, Bill Barksdale, Max Symmes, Philip J. Reed, Robert Bowling, Jason Morales, Keith Charles, and Asher Henderson.

ALSO FROM BOSS FIGHT BOOKS